3-INGREDIENT
SLOW COOKER
RECIPES

3-INGREDIENT
SLOW COOKER
RECIPES

200 Recipes for Memorable Meals

SUZANNE BONET

FAIR WINDS
PRESS
GLOUCESTER, MASSACHUSETTS

Text © 2005 by Suzanne Bonet

First published in the USA in 2005 by
Fair Winds Press, a member of
Quayside Publishing Group
33 Commercial Street
Gloucester, MA 01930

09 08 07 06 05   2 3 4 5

ISBN 1-59233-180-7

Library of Congress Cataloging-in-Publication Data available

Cover design by Ariana Dingman
Cover illustration by Jessica Allen
Book design by Leslie Haimes

Printed and bound in Canada

The information in this book is for educational purposes only. It is not intended to
replace the advice of a physician or medical practitioner. Please see your health care
provider before beginning any new diet or health program.

This book is dedicated to the memories of

my mother and brother, whom I deeply miss;

to my daughters, Christina and Clarissa;

and to my sweetheart, Jim.

My motivation to perfect the quick-and-easy

slow-cooker recipe stemmed from my desire to

spend more time with all of you.

Contents

Introduction

"Chic" is a term wholly dissociated from the slow cooker, yet the popularity of the lowly slow cooker is on the upswing. A growing health-consciousness and desire to simplify are *lifestyle* reasons for the slow cooker's rediscovery.

But other reasons exist, too. What's nicer than coming home to the aroma of Rosemary-Lamb Stew (page 127) or Gingered Pineapple Chicken (page 149) after a long day away? Cheaper cuts of meat taste tender and moist after slow cooking, and this helps with the budgetary stresses felt by graduate students, young adults, and growing families. Time-stressed households want to eat in, but they don't want freezer food, pizza, and microwave-centered meals day after day. They yearn for the flavorful, home-prepared variety. Everyone today seems to be strapped for time and money and togetherness. Yes, everyone is on the lookout for flavorful yet simple foods whose preparation doesn't take time away from family, school, career, or hobbies.

So, it's time to scramble to the back of the pantry and retrieve the appliance you've been snubbing, being a person of high culinary goals. Don't look now, but cheaper cuts of meat are suddenly chic at the country's best restaurants. It seems everyone is discovering that lamb shanks, pot roast, and brisket are mighty tasty when cooked right, and we're here to help you figure out how to do that.

Why just three ingredients? Because the recipes in this collection were selected to ensure that the slow cooker is utilized as intended—as an appliance that makes your life easier, simpler, less costly, and more satisfying. The problem with most slow-cooker recipes is that they expect too much from you. They require lots of ingredients and steps before you "fix it and forget it." Not the recipes in this collection. These truly are simple recipes, featuring only three ingredients, not counting water, salt, and black pepper. Best of all, these recipes are memorable, not mushy!

Chapter 1

•••

Getting to Know Your Slow Cooker

Slow Cooker Types, Sizes, Features, and Safety

Slow cookers were introduced in the 1970s, and to date, more than 100 million have been sold. The Crock-Pot was the original slow cooker, and it still makes up 85 percent of the market. The catchy brand name, belonging to the Rival Company, became synonymous with the slow cooker. Today, we may still forget and call slow cookers by the wrong name, but that doesn't change the facts: All Crock-Pots are slow cookers, but not all slow cookers are Crock-Pot brand. Cuisinart, Farberware, Hamilton Beach, West Bend, and many other companies manufacture slow cookers as well.

What exactly is a slow cooker? It's a small, stand-alone appliance that cooks food slowly in a ceramic pot. The slow cooker's heating element surrounds the food with heat, so that the food cooks evenly. This eliminates the need to stir the cooking food, making its preparation extremely convenient for the cook. Some slow cooker-type appliances have heat coils on the bottom only, as well as adjustable thermostats. These are not true slow cookers, however. If you have this type of cooker, refer to your product manual for advice on how to adapt the recipes in this cookbook.

When first introduced, slow cookers came with two settings, LOW and HIGH, which most slow cookers still have. The exact temperatures of these settings vary by manufacturer, but LOW is generally about 200°F (90°C) and HIGH is about 300°F (150°C). These temperatures, though low in comparison to those used in conventional cooking, exceed food-safety standards.

For most slow-cooker recipes, it's possible to set the slow cooker to LOW and leave it unattended for the length of the recommended cooking time. But while the cooking times are flexible, it is possible that unexpected delays—getting stuck in a major traffic jam, for instance—could result in overcooked food. Many of the newer slow cookers therefore are programmable and often come with a WARM temperature setting, which is approximately 140°F (60°C), to prevent overcooking and to keep food at a safe temperature for up to four hours. This feature is also convenient if you want to hold foods at serving temperature for late-arriving family members or at potluck gatherings.

Even if you have a basic slow cooker with only a LOW and a HIGH temperature setting, the Rival Company sells a remarkable device called the Smart-Part Module. This little item works like a timer. Just insert the plug of your slow cooker into the module and set the cooking time. The module will automatically switch your slow cooker to WARM when your meal is finished cooking. It works with any brand of slow cooker that has a ceramic pot and that is rated 400 watts (3.3 amps) or less.

Slow Cookers and Bacteria

The slow cooker's lengthy cooking time, its direct heat, and the steam locked inside the pot thanks to its tight-fitting lid all work in concert to destroy bacteria when commonsense food-handling procedures are followed. In the 1970s, when slow cookers were first introduced, some people unknowingly practiced unsafe food-handling procedures and promoted the growth of enough bacteria in their slow-cooked food to cause illness. These days, slow cookers operate at higher temperatures, killing bacteria faster and better. In addition, the kitchen seems to have been affected by the post–September 11 safety revolution. Now everybody is all about practicing safety—including food safety.

Although most slow-cooker food-safety practices are common sense, you probably need to refresh your memory. So, take a peek at the food-safety tips on page 15. You'll be glad you did.

The Basic Slow Cooker

When shopping for a new slow cooker, it's easy to become overwhelmed by the many types of cookers and variety of features available. Therefore, it's useful to understand the components of a basic slow cooker.

A basic slow cooker consists of an electric cooking pot with two temperature settings, LOW and HIGH. The pot is usually made of stoneware and is inserted in a base that contains the heating element, although less-expensive slow cookers can be single units and may even have only one temperature setting. If the cooking pot is removable, it often can be washed in the dishwasher, although you should consult your manufacturer's instructions to be sure. Some stoneware pots have an unfinished, porous bottom, which is fine for cooking but not for washing in the dishwasher. A removable cooking pot can also double as a serving dish. Even the basic slow cooker generally has a tempered glass lid to allow easy viewing of the cooking food, and often has handles that stay cool and are designed for easy gripping.

Slow-Cooker Features and Sizes

Beyond the basics is a dizzying array of special features. Some slow cookers are fully programmable. One model has a divided pot to cook two recipes at the same time. Another model is entirely cool to the touch, even when cooking on HIGH. Many come with a feature that automatically switches the unit to a temperature that safely keeps food warm once the cooking time has elapsed. A designer-style slow cooker makes an especially pretty appearance at the dinner table, doubling as an elegant serving dish. With some, the cooking pot goes from the base to the stovetop, oven, refrigerator, or freezer. A few even have nonstick interiors, and some have blinking lights that signal if the power went off during the cooking time. Even without all of these improvements, however, the basic slow cooker is more than adequate for preparing and serving a delightfully tasty and convenient meal.

Slow cookers come in a variety of sizes, from 1 quart, perfect for dips, to 6 $^{1}/_{2}$ quarts, great for large quantities, roasts, and large birds. Since slow cookers cook best and most safely when they're at least half full of food and no more than two-thirds full, the quantity that you typically cook should determine the size of slow cooker you purchase. Generally, a 3½- to 5-quart slow cooker is the best option for the average household.

Checklist of Slow-Cooker Features

If you don't already have a slow cooker, or if you're in the market for a new one, here are a few things to think about before you make your purchase.

What size slow cooker would be best for your needs?

- 1 quart, if you'll primarily be making dips and sauces.
- 3½ to 4 quarts, if you'll be cooking for 4 or fewer people.
- 5 to 6½ quarts or larger, if you'll be cooking for 5 or more people or if you like leftovers.

What shape slow cooker would be better for you?

- Round, the standard shape, if you'll be making a variety of recipes.
- Oval, if you'll be cooking a lot of roasts and whole chickens.

What other basic design features would be beneficial?

- A removable insert, if you'd like to serve your food directly from the slow cooker or put the cooking container in the dishwasher.
- A nonstick pot, to make cleanup easier.
- A lightweight slow cooker or removable pot, to keep the unit light enough to safely handle. Stoneware pots are heavy to begin with and can become very heavy when filled with food. Some slow cookers are made of aluminum, which is much lighter than stoneware.
- A decorative unit, if your slow cooker will be doubling as a serving dish. Slow-cooker exteriors are now made of stainless steel and come in solid colors, but you can still get units decorated with ivy and other kitchen motifs.

Which bells and whistles are worth the added cost for you?

- A WARM setting, the most practical feature not included on basic slow cookers, is worthwhile if you tend to return home later than expected.

- The cool-to-the-touch feature is important if you have little fingers around the house that could get burned.

- An aluminum pot insert is helpful if you prefer to sear meat before cooking it and would like to do so in the slow cooker rather than on the stove. The aluminum insert can also double as a griddle.

- A programmable temperature control is useful if you need flexibility. According to the U.S. Department of Agriculture, slow cookers are safe when used exclusively on LOW, but some cooks prefer to cook on HIGH for an hour, then reduce the temperature to LOW, and finally switch it to WARM once the food is done. This shortens the time that food is between 40°F (4°C) and 140°F (60°C), the temperature range in which bacteria multiply most rapidly. This method also shortens the cooking time slightly without hurting the slow-cooked flavor.

- An electronic database of recipes is helpful if you like to experiment. Before purchasing a unit with this feature, make sure you can read the LED screen, which by necessity is small.

Some slow cookers also come with accessories such as a dust cover, travel case, and meat rack. Some of these items are universal and can be purchased separate from the slow cooker, but not all are. For help in determining what accessories come with the different slow cookers currently on the market, see "Resources for Slow Cooking" on page 246.

Slow-Cooker Safety

Once you have chosen the appropriate slow cooker for your needs and preferences, you have to learn how to cook safely with it. Be certain to consult your manufacturer's instruction booklet and follow all the safety recommendations. Here are a few of the more frequently cited safety precautions.

- *Do not submerge the base of the slow cooker in water.* In addition, before putting the removable pot or insert in the microwave, on the stovetop, in the oven, or in the broiler, make sure it can be used that way. If the directions don't explicitly state that something can be done with the slow cooker, be safe and don't do it.

- *Do not preheat the slow cooker, and never turn it on unless it has food in it.* The temperature gap between a hot slow cooker and cold food may cause a crack or, at the very least, may cause food to stick to or burn in the pot.

- *Do not put cold water in a hot slow-cooker pot.* The pot may crack. Wait until the pot has cooled to wash it.

- *Do not use a chipped or cracked ceramic pot.* Not only is a damaged pot impossible to wash thoroughly, but it may also fall apart at the worst possible time—while you're cooking.

- *Think twice before filling an insert away from the base.* Most slow cookers have crockery inserts, which can be heavy even when empty. Adding food increases the weight, raising the risk of dropping the insert or spilling its contents while trying to insert it into the slow cooker.

- *Follow common sense when storing foods in the slow cooker.* Sometimes, of course, you'll want to prepare slow-cooker ingredients in advance, and that may mean storing a few of the ingredients in the crockery insert and stowing the insert in the refrigerator overnight. If you do this, keep any meat separate from the vegetables and other ingredients until it's time to cook them. You should never allow meat juices to touch other ingredients except during cooking. In addition, if you fill the insert the night before, you may find that potatoes or fruit become discolored or pasta or rice absorb too much liquid.

- *Never store leftovers or reheat food in the slow cooker.* Bacteria multiply quickly under certain temperature conditions. Instead, divide large amounts of leftovers among several small, shallow containers, then stow the containers in the refrigerator. This will allow even the center of the food in each container to cool down quickly enough to prevent bacteria growth. The danger zone for food is between 40°F (4°C) and 140°F (60°C), the temperature range in which bacteria can multiply quickly in food, causing the potential for food-borne illness. Never allow food to be in the danger zone for more than two hours.

- *Learn how to use a kitchen thermometer.* It's one of the most useful kitchen gadgets you'll find. According to the Partnership for Food Safety Education (www.fightbac.org/pdf/cook.pdf), you can be sure that foods are thoroughly cooked when they reach the following temperatures:

>Beef roasts, 145°F (60°C) (medium rare) or
> 160°F (70°C)(medium)
>
>Ground beef, 160°F (70°C)
>
>Raw sausages, 160°F (70°C)
>
>Ready-to-eat sausages, 165°F (75°C)
>
>Pork roasts, pork chops, ground pork, 160°F (70°C) (medium)
> or 170°F (80°C) (well done)
>
>Whole poultry, 180°F (85°C)
>
>Chicken breasts, 170°F (80°C)
>
>Leftovers, 165°F (75°C)

- *Do not serve food from a slow cooker that was accidentally shut off for a period of time during cooking.* If you come home and find your clocks blinking, throw out the food in your slow cooker even if it looks well cooked. You most likely will have no idea how long the electricity was out and whether or not the food temperature was in the danger zone for too long. If you are present when the electricity goes out, finish cooking the food on your gas stove or find a friend or relative with a working stove.

While slow-cooker safety is important, it's also important that your finished dishes look appealing and taste even better. In the next chapter, you'll find tips and techniques for individual foods and food groups.

• •

Chapter 2

Using Your Slow Cooker

Slow-Cooker Basics

This cookbook contains 200 easy and tasty recipes, but you can convert many of your favorite conventional recipes for use with the slow cooker if you follow a few basic rules. The following guidelines will also ensure your success with recipes specifically designed for the slow cooker.

Meat and Poultry

Unquestionably great in the slow cooker are roasts, ham, ground beef, sausage, and whole and cut-up chicken. Throw them in the pot and go, as long as you understand these guidelines.

- *Buy roasts, hams, and birds that fit inside your slow cooker with some headroom to spare.* Slow cookers should be at least half full for the contents to cook properly, yet should never have less than a generous inch of space at the top. Turkey bones poking at the lid is also a no-no, since the lid must close well to seal in the moisture and flavor. Overfilling the slow cooker with liquid is sure to produce a sloppy mishap when the food reaches the simmering point.

- *Opt for inexpensive and lean cuts of meat.* Buying a beautifully marbled roast is more than unnecessary for taste and tenderness when slow cooking—it's a waste of money. The moist, gentle heat of the slow cooker will transform even the leanest, toughest cuts into tender morsels.

- *Trim all visible fat, even from lean meat.* You don't need the extra fat calories, and the slow cooker doesn't need the help.

- *Remove poultry skin only if you prefer.* Some people prefer the skin left on, claiming that the meat is more tender and succulent when cooked that way. Others prefer the skin removed before cooking to reduce the fat and calories. As long as there is sufficient liquid to cover the meat, cooking it with the skin on is unnecessary. Whether to consume the cooked skin or not is a personal preference.
- *Precook ground meat and sausage.* This will render out the fat before the meat is added to the slow cooker. The only time you shouldn't precook ground meat or sausage is when you're making meatloaf or the like. For meatloaf, choose an extra-lean grade for the healthiest preparation.
- *When filling the slow cooker, put the vegetables on the bottom and the meat on the top.* This is because meat cooks faster than vegetables. Until you're familiar with how they cook in your pot, check meats and poultry for doneness after 6 or 7 hours on LOW, even if the recipe states a cooking range of 8 to 10 hours. Check sooner if the cooking range given is 4 or 5 hours.

Fish and Shellfish

This category of food is relatively new to the slow cooker, but with proper handling, you can enjoy tasty and healthful fish and shellfish dishes with no muss or fuss.

- *Use firm fishes such as cod, catfish, haddock, salmon, and tuna in your dishes.* Don't substitute more delicate fishes such as flounder, which won't hold up through extended periods of cooking.
- *Add shellfish towards the end of cooking, according to the recipe instructions.* Shrimp, scallops, and minced clams toughen if they're overcooked.

Vegetables

Vegetables pair well with meat to make one-pot meals, stews, and soups, but there are a few things you need to know.

- *Add greens and less dense or strongly flavored vegetables during the last 20 to 60 minutes of cooking.* Cruciferous vegetables, for instance, need to be cooked for the longest periods of time, whereas leafy vegetables, such as spinach and kale, will cook in the brief time it takes them to warm up to the temperature of the surrounding food. Depending on the quantity of vegetables added, the temperature of the pot will dip for a time. Take this into consideration when timing how long it will take for the food to finish cooking. The more vegetables you add, the longer it will be before your dinner is ready for the table.

- *Chop vegetables into pieces or chunks of uniform size for even cooking.* In most cases, vegetable pieces should be no more than an inch or so thick. The smaller the chunks, the faster they will cook. If you would prefer your slow cooker to cook for 10 hours, you can chop your vegetables a smidgeon larger than if you want to get dinner on the table in 8 hours sharp.

Rice, Barley, Pasta, and Beans

Rice, barley, pasta, and beans often accompany meat in the slow cooker, but each has its own special requirements for cooking.

- *Use raw long-grain rice over quick-cooking rice, pearl barley over quick-cooking barley, and brown or wild rice over white rice.* They require more time to cook, which makes them more convenient. The fact that they're more flavorful and nutritious is a bonus. Pearl barley and brown rice take approximately two to four times longer to cook than their more processed counterparts. Wild rice, which is really a variety of grass and not a rice at all, takes even longer to cook.

- *Add uncooked pasta to the pot during the last 1 to 2 hours of cooking to avoid overcooking.* Alternatively, cook the pasta on the stove, drain it, and add it during the last 5 to 15 minutes of cooking, although you lose convenience and flavor this way. Cook pasta until it's al dente and no softer, as it may continue to cook in the pot. You can use this method for barley and rice, too, but again, you'll sacrifice some convenience and flavor.

- *Use canned or precooked beans and legumes for convenience.* Uncooked dried beans take much longer to cook. For maximum tenderness, do not add sweet or salty foods, or acidic foods such as tomatoes, until the other foods in the recipe are fully cooked or close to it.

Dairy Products

Dairy products contribute much to the taste of a slow-cooked dish, but they, too, have special requirements.

- *Stir natural cheese, sour cream, yogurt, milk, cream, and soy products into the pot immediately before serving.* The same goes for rice milk and nut milks. Continue cooking only until the cheese has melted or the sauce is thoroughly heated. Dairy products and the like may separate and appear to curdle if cooked for about an hour—and certainly when cooked longer.

- *Use pasteurized processed cheese, canned evaporated skim milk, and nonfat dry milk in recipes that call for extended cooking times.* These processed dairy products hold up to heat beautifully without separating.

- *Opt for canned condensed cream soups over ready-to-eat soups.* They're processed and very stable for slow cooking.

Flavorings, Herbs, Spices, and Garnishes

Properly flavoring and garnishing food will help your meals come out of the slow cooker tasting simply fabulous.

- *Use sugar, brown sugar, maple syrup, and the like without reservation.* They add flavor with no downside in slow cooking, other than the calories.

- *Consider carefully when selecting a sugar substitute for your slow-cooker recipe.* Splenda (sucralose) is heat-stable plus has no aftertaste. Even though Sweet'N Low (saccharine), Sweet One (acesulfame-k), and stevia are heat-stable, they often leave a slight aftertaste. Aspartame formulations such as NutraSweet and Equal are not heat-stable, and although they have no aftertaste, they are not recommended because they lose sweetness after extended heating.

- *Expect slow-cooked flavorings and spices to have different characteristics than you're used to.* Slow cooking increases the flavor intensity of peppers and bay leaves, for instance. On the other hand, it tends to cause onion, ground cinnamon, and other ground spices to lose flavor. Many slow-cooker recipes, therefore, specify whole herbs and spices, which you can tie together in a piece of cheesecloth and add to the pot. In the absence of whole spices in your pantry, add ground herbs and spices near the end of cooking.

- *Garnish your meals to offset the fading that slow-cooked foods may experience.* Add visual appeal with some grated cheese, a dollop of sour cream, or a sprinkle of chopped fresh or dried parsley, cilantro, chives, tomatoes, or green peppers.

Baked Goods

You may be surprised that you can bake in your slow cooker, but it's true. Some slow cookers come with a covered baking unit and a rack. If yours didn't, improvise.

- *If your slow cooker didn't come with a baking unit, use any oven-safe pan.* Pyrex bakeware or a large coffee can will also work.
- *For recipes that require a lid on the baking pan or unit, use any oven-safe lid.* If you don't have an oven-safe lid, try 5 to 6 layers of paper toweling.
- *Use the slow-cooker lid in addition to the baking-pan lid, unless the recipe specifically states otherwise.*
- *Always use a rack when the recipe calls for one.* If your slow cooker didn't come with one, use any oven-safe rack. A rack elevates the pan off the floor of the slow cooker to provide circulation for even baking.
- *When adapting recipes for the slow cooker, always remember that the baking times for baked goods must be doubled or quadrupled.*

As you can see, the slow cooker is a versatile small appliance—just about everything can be prepared in it. Whether you're an expert or just starting to learn about slow cooking, you will prepare excellent food if you follow the simple guidelines in this chapter. Convert favorite family recipes or enjoy one of the quick-and-easy recipes in this cookbook. Either way you create wonderful dishes with minimal effort.

Even shopping to stock the pantry can require just minimal effort. In the next chapter, you'll see what foods to keep on hand so that you're always prepared to make a slow-cooker meal that's table-ready with very little work.

Chapter 3

• •

Stocking Your Slow-Cooker Pantry

The Foods That Help Your Slow Cooker Make Your Life Easier

A certain segment of society would have us believe that only from-scratch-and-all-natural constitutes genuine home cooking. That's all well and good, except that if we don't have the time to slave over the stove every night, we certainly don't have the time to make Worcestershire sauce from scratch. It makes sense, then, for the well-stocked slow-cooker pantry to contain a variety of prepared foods that enhance meat, poultry, beans, and other meal fixings. This makes it a cinch to fill your slow cooker and come home later to a fragrant, delicious meal that's table-ready—and isn't that our goal?

Note that your angst concerning the use of frozen and canned food can also be laid to rest. Frozen and canned vegetables and fruits are processed immediately after harvest, before they lose nutrients. Fresh produce, on the other hand, loses nutrients on the way to the grocery store. So, never feel guilty again about using frozen or canned foods. Because of the quick processing, they're often more nutritious than fresh fruits and veggies.

Prepared spice and herb mixes are not only convenient, but also economical. Spices have a shelf life of about six months, so buying individual spices can be an exercise in futility, since they are almost always used in scant quantity. When you buy mixed herbs and spices, you're more likely to use the entire bottle before the contents lose flavor. This holds true for other seasonings and flavorings as well. How many times have you purchased a special ingredient for one recipe, only to have it languish in the refrigerator or spice rack until it was past its prime? So, cooking with prepared foods saves you time and money, and in many cases, it increases the nutritional content of your food. How can you argue with that?

We're fortunate that supermarkets stock more than the basics these days. Canned tomatoes, for instance, come in fifty-four varieties at one national grocery store. Anyone can find mushroom soup condensed, dried, flavored as golden mushroom soup, combined with chicken, and probably in other ways as well. Each of these products contributes a unique blend of seasonings and flavorings to your slow-cooker recipes without your having to stock the individual flavorings and take the time to measure them out.

The Slow-Cooker Pantry, Refrigerator, and Freezer

While it's difficult in a cookbook to take into account every reader's taste preferences, here is a general list of ingredients to consider keeping on hand. All the ingredients listed work well in the slow cooker, and many are available preseasoned, which saves time and money. Start by purchasing the nonperishables that you love, and add others to your pantry as your budget allows. Because there are so many varieties and flavors of many of these products available, it's impossible to list every one. As a rule of thumb, when you're shopping without a specific recipe in mind, grab the can of seasoned tomato sauce, for instance, that is the most appealing to your taste buds.

BAKING SUPPLIES

All-purpose baking mix

Baking chocolate, unsweetened

Cake mixes, variety

Cornstarch

Flour

DAIRY PRODUCTS

Butter, salted and/or unsalted

Cheese, cream

Cheese, Parmesan, grated

Cheeses, shredded, variety

Eggs

Milk, condensed

Milk, evaporated

DRESSINGS, SAUCES, SOUPS

Bouillon, beef, chicken, and vegetable

Broth, beef, chicken, and vegetable

Dressings, variety

Glazes, variety

Marinades, variety

Pasta sauce

Soups, condensed cream of
mushroom, chicken, and celery

Teriyaki sauce

Tomato paste

Tomato sauce

FLAVORINGS, SEASONINGS

Bay leaves

Black peppercorns (and a grinder)

Chili mix, dry

Chili sauce

Corn syrup

Dressing mixes, dry, variety

Honey

Hot sauce

Italian seasoning
(recipe on page 29)

Ketchup

Maple syrup, pure

Mustard, Dijon

Mustard, yellow, prepared

Salt, iodized or sea

Soup mixes, dry, variety

Soy sauce

Sugar, brown, light and/or dark

Sugar, cinnamon
(recipe on page 29)

Sugar, vanilla (recipe on page 29)

Sugar, white

Tabasco sauce

Worcestershire sauce

FRUITS

Fruits, canned, variety

Fruits, dried, variety

Pie fillings, canned, variety

Jams and preserves, variety

LEGUMES, PASTA, RICE

Chick peas, canned

Kidney beans, canned

Pasta, dry, variety

Rice, converted, raw

White beans, canned

MEAT, POULTRY, FISH

Beef, ground

Beef brisket

Beef pot roast

Chicken, canned

Chicken, whole

Chicken breasts

Chicken legs

Chicken wings

Pork chops

Pork roast

Ribs

Salmon, fresh

Salmon, canned

Sausages

Stew meat

Tuna, canned

NUTS

Almond halves

Mixed nuts

Pecan halves

Peanuts, shelled

Walnut halves

OIL, VINEGAR

Cooking spray

Oil, olive

Vinegar, apple cider

Vinegar, balsamic

Vinegar, white

VEGETABLES

Carrots, baby and regular,
fresh or frozen

Celery, fresh or frozen

Chiles, canned

Corn, canned

Corn blends, canned

Mushrooms, fresh or dried

Onions, fresh or frozen

Potatoes, hash brown, frozen

Potatoes, white, fresh or frozen

Salsa, fresh or canned

Sweet potatoes, fresh or canned

Tomatoes, crushed, canned

Tomatoes, whole, canned or dried

Vegetables, mixed, frozen

Vegetables, seasoning-blend, frozen (recipe
on page 30)

Vegetables, stew, frozen

Slow-Cooker Seasoning and Flavoring Mixes

It's possible to create seasoning and flavoring mixes at home in addition to purchasing them at the store. You can find recipes for many mixes, but here are a few that are especially popular (and that you'll find in recipes throughout this book). Feel free to adjust the proportions of the ingredients according to your taste.

🧂 Cinnamon Sugar

1/2 cup (100 g) granulated sugar

2 tablespoons (14 g) ground cinnamon

Put the sugar and cinnamon in a small bowl and stir to combine. Store the mixture in an airtight container in a cool place.

🧂 Vanilla Sugar

2 cups (100 g, or 50 g) granulated or powdered sugar

1 vanilla bean

Put the sugar in an airtight container, then push the vanilla bean down into the sugar until it's completely submerged. Let the sugar with the vanilla bean sit undisturbed for 1 to 2 weeks, then remove the bean. Store the mixture in the airtight container in a cool place.

🧂 Italian Seasoning

1 teaspoon dried oregano

1 teaspoon dried basil

1 teaspoon dried rosemary

1 teaspoon dried thyme

1 teaspoon dried marjoram

1 teaspoon dried sage

1 teaspoon dried savory

Put the oregano, basil, rosemary, thyme, marjoram, sage, and savory in a small bowl and stir to combine. Store the mixture in an airtight container in a cool place.

🧂 Seasoning-Blend Vegetables

3 onions

2 stalks celery

1 green pepper

1 red pepper

Dice the onions, and cut the celery, green pepper, and red pepper into chunks of uniform size. Place the chopped vegetables in a plastic freezer bag, and store them in the freezer until you need them for a recipe. Note that you may wish to prepare mixtures of different-sized vegetables for different uses, or freeze a variety of amounts for different recipes.

A Final Note

The most important thing to remember when stocking your pantry is that great ingredients and flavor combinations make for great food. Always buy the highest quality products, as well as the flavor combinations that appeal to your taste buds. It's never a good idea to buy a brand or flavor that you don't like just because it's on sale. If a recipe calls for a garlic-flavored sauce and you always pass on the garlic, you're better off using a different-flavored sauce. Likewise, never cook with wine or spirits that you wouldn't drink by the glass. Follow this rule faithfully, and you'll be rewarded with fabulous tasting food every time.

Now that your pantry is stocked, let's get to the good stuff—the recipes that will make your life easier and your taste buds happy. It's time to turn the page and discover quick, easy recipes for slow-cooker foods—with just three ingredients or fewer!

Chapter 4

• •

Before You Begin

Information and Guidelines for Slow-Cooking Success

Master chefs need read no further. But everyone else may want to learn what's what on a recipe page in this cookbook and peruse a short list of slow-cooking tips and techniques. As my grandmother always used to say, "Knowledge is power." In this case, it's also success in the kitchen.

The Parts of the Recipe

It's always a good idea to read a recipe through at least once before you start. That way, you'll know what ingredients to have on hand, how long the recipe should take to prepare and cook, and if your slow cooker needs any special attention during cooking. The recipes in this cookbook are set up to make this step easy for you. When reviewing a recipe, you'll find the usual—a list of ingredients, directions, and a cooking time range. You'll also discover a few other useful tidbits of information.

- *Ingredient list and directions.* These two items are an indispensable part of every recipe. This cookbook lists the ingredients in the order they're used and includes their metric equivalents. Before starting, make sure you have all the ingredients required. Perhaps it's not a bad idea to place everything on a countertop, to be really sure. With only three or fewer ingredients (not counting salt, black pepper, and water) in every recipe, no one's counter is too small for this step. It may even prevent false starts caused by unknowingly being out of or short of a pantry staple.

- *Yield.* Are you cooking in empty-nester quantities or entertaining a crowd? Do you just love leftovers, or do you abhor them? The yield information makes it a snap to choose a recipe to suit any occasion. Given that we're all watching portion sizes these days, the serving sizes in these recipes are not overly conservative, but they're also not on the large side (unless they're specified as generous). Take particularly small or large appetites into consideration here.

- *Tip.* Most of the recipes in this cookbook are simple and straight-forward. But just in case, some of the recipes include tips about an ingredient or cooking technique. Need to know how to do something? Look for a tip with the recipe.

- *Add it!* This is actually the second item you may want to check after the ingredient list and directions. It offers variations or additional ingredients for days when you want to enjoy a little variety or spice. When you have the time and inclination, these little twists may be just the ticket.

- *Note.* Protein, carb, and calorie counts don't tell the whole story about many of the foods we eat. The notes with many of the recipes in this cookbook offer interesting tidbits about nutrition and ingredients. Read 'em, skip 'em, or exploit your newfound knowledge at the trivia game table. It's up to you.

- *Cooking time and Attention.* These items provide vital information at a glance. They make it easy to choose a recipe that fits the amount of time you have available for cooking the food. These items also eliminate unwelcome surprises—for instance, starting a recipe that needs to be stirred during cooking when you were planning to be gone all day. Recipes labeled as needing minimal attention are the fix it-and-forget-it type. All the other recipes have the briefest of summaries to explain their attention requirements. If you see anything other than "Minimal" listed for the attention required, you'll know to read the recipe directions for more information.

- *Nutritional analysis.* If you're on a diet or have a medical condition, check the very bottom of the recipe for the number of calories and grams of fat, protein, carbohydrate, and dietary fiber found in one average serving of the basic recipe.

Slow-Cooking Tips and Techniques

Now that you know what's included in the recipes in this cookbook, it's time to look at the slow-cooker tips and techniques that are essential for making good decisions when cooking. Slow cooking is different from conventional cooking, and while it doesn't demand an excess of talent, it does require you to know a few things. Apply the following tips and techniques to every recipe, and you'll enjoy slow-cooker success.

• Just like recipes for conventional cooking, the recipes in this cookbook provide a range of cooking times to account for variables such as the initial temperatures of the ingredients, room temperature, altitude, and variations in the temperature settings among the different slow-cooker models. Once you become accustomed to your slow cooker and have tried a recipe a few times, you'll have an idea of whether or not your food is apt to be done at the beginning or end of the given time range. This also helps you decide if it's appropriate to leave the slow cooker on unattended. You'll have a good idea of how much wiggle time you have if you become unexpectedly delayed and can't turn off the slow cooker when expected.

• Manufacturers recommend that slow cookers be between one-half and two-thirds full. An underfilled slow cooker may become too hot and burn the food, while an overfilled slow cooker may take too long to reach a safe temperature, increasing the potential for bacteria growth. Choose the properly sized slow cooker for each recipe, and don't double or halve a recipe unless your slow cooker can handle it. For more information on slow-cooker safety, see "Resources for Slow Cooking" on page 246.

• Most of the recipes in this cookbook do not require the meat to be browned because this is an added step. If you prefer the flavor and look of browned meat, however, sear your meat in a skillet with a little olive oil before placing it in the slow cooker. Just be aware that browned meat may shorten the cooking time slightly, since when you brown the meat, you're starting the cooking process.

• Never lift the slow-cooker lid during cooking unless instructed to do so. If you can't see inside the slow cooker because of condensation on the lid, jiggle the lid to make the droplets fall back into the cooker. Because slow cookers cook foods evenly and with moist heat, taking the lid off to stir or to monitor food is unnecessary and frequently counterproductive. In extreme situations, lifting the lid too much may cause your food to dry out. If this happens, add a few tablespoons of water or other liquid to correct the situation. More of a problem, however, is that lifting the lid will cause the temperature in the slow cooker to drop 10 to 15 degrees, which will take between 15 and 25 minutes to regain.

If you lift the lid, you'll have to cook the food longer. How much longer will depend on when you lift the lid during the cooking process and for how long. If you lift the lid at the very beginning or end of cooking, you won't need to add as much cooking time as you would if you peek during the middle of cooking, when the food is at its highest temperature and needs the accumulated heat to finish cooking.

It's hard to provide a rule of thumb for the many possibilities—from when a lid is accidentally knocked off the pot for a second or two, to when your child tries to help by removing the lid and stirring until you notice there's mischief afoot. The best solution is to add at least 15 minutes to the recommended cooking time and to use your best judgment or a meat thermometer to test your food for doneness at the end of the cooking time.

- Always taste a finished dish before serving it so you can adjust the seasonings if necessary. Long cooking can increase the intensity of some seasonings and decrease it in others. Many of the recipes in this cookbook use time-saving, prepared ingredients with varying amounts of salt and flavorings. Therefore, it's best to season a dish to taste once it's fully cooked. Many of the recipes include specific recommendations for seasonings and flavorings to punch up the dish.

As you can see, slow cooking is a method without difficult or time-intensive techniques. It's just that simple. You are now armed with the knowledge and the power to prepare a wide variety of foods the slow-cooker way. So, what are you waiting for? It's time to turn the page and discover 200 delicious ways to make cooking a quick-and-easy pleasure—with just three or fewer ingredients.

Multi-Ingredient Products and Convenience

Three-ingredient speed and convenience often require the use of multi-ingredient products to give dishes deliciously complex flavors. The vast majority of these multi-ingredient products are manufactured by familiar national companies. Take a look, and you'll soon notice that multi-ingredient products are in vogue. The supermarket shelves are crowded with them:

- Tomato and pasta sauces with added flavorings such as garlic, onion, mushroom, and wine

- Soups, gravies, and seasonings with gourmet twists

- Sauces and marinades with garlic, herb, chili, or citrus flavorings

- Frozen and canned vegetable blends and dressed-up potatoes

- Shredded cheese blends, sometimes with added spices

Many of the recipes in this cookbook use multi-ingredient products, with the brand name included in the ingredient list if it's a hard-to-find or one-of-a-kind product. Even when a brand name is mentioned, feel free to make a substitution. The slow cooker is meant to free you from the drudgery of cooking. Shopping for pantry items should never be a chore, and trudging around town hunting for ingredients is contrary to the spirit of this cookbook.

Should you prefer to search out the few one-of-a-kind ingredients unavailable in your local grocery store, head for a large city supermarket, specialty or gourmet shop, or even the Internet. What you'll discover while shopping at these specialty stores or surfing the web may evolve into a three-ingredient recipe sensation of your own.

Chapter 5

• •

Breakfast

Kick-start your day the night before. Throw a few ingredients into your slow cooker before you go to bed, and wake up to the sweet, nutty aroma of Banana-Nut Oatmeal (page 42) or Breakfast Apple Crunch (page 39). As it turns out, breakfast really is the most important meal of the day. Researchers have found that skipping breakfast increases the risks of developing diabetes, becoming obese, and even having a heart attack. People who consume whole-grain cereals and fruits for breakfast receive the greatest health benefits. The slow cooker is especially suitable for preparing oatmeal and fruit, as well as other breakfast favorites, so go for it tonight and enjoy a great start to your day tomorrow!

# Basic Granola

Cooking time: 2 1/2 to 3 1/2 hours   **Attention:** Stir every 30 minutes

Basic granola—or designer granola! Keep this recipe simple for a plain but delicious granola, or pump it up with antioxidants by tossing in your favorite combination of dried fruits, nuts, and seeds.

   4 cups (300 g) old-fashioned **rolled oats**

   1/2 cup (113 g) **honey** or **maple syrup**

   3 tablespoons (45 ml) **vegetable oil**, enriched with vitamin E, if desired

Spray the inside of the slow cooker with cooking spray.

Put the rolled oats, honey, and vegetable oil in the slow cooker and mix well. Partially cover, propping the lid open with a twist of foil or a wooden skewer to allow the moisture to escape, and cook on LOW for 2 1/2 to 3 1/2 hours, or until the oat morsels are roasted dry and golden brown, stirring every 30 minutes.

Allow the granola to cool, then transfer it to an airtight container. Store it in the refrigerator.

YIELD: 5 servings

ADD IT! When the granola has cooled, add in a total of 1 to 2 cups of raisins, shredded unsweetened coconut, chopped walnuts, slivered almonds, or shelled pumpkin or sunflower seeds. Mix and match your favorites!

NOTE: It's not easy to get a full day's requirement of vitamin E through food sources. Fortunately, manufacturers are starting to enrich vegetable oil with vitamin E. Enriched oil is a smart way to get your E because the body absorbs this fat-soluble vitamin best when it's consumed along with foods containing a fat such as vegetable oil. Vitamin E and vegetable oil—it's a natural!

NUTRITIONAL ANALYSIS: One serving of the basic recipe contains 390 calories; 12 g fat; 10 g protein; 62 g carbohydrate; and 7 g dietary fiber.

Breakfast Apple Crunch

Cooking time: 5 to 6 hours on LOW, 2 to 3 hours on HIGH
Attention: Minimal

Apple Crunch for breakfast is appealing when the weather turns cold. The crunchy topping makes it all the more satisfying.

> One 21-ounce (595-g) can cinnamon-and-spice **apple pie filling**
>
> 2 cups (244 g) Basic **Granola** (page 38) plus a smidge more for garnish
>
> 1/2 cup (60 ml) water
>
> 4 tablespoons (56 g) lightly salted **butter**, cut into pieces

Spray the inside of the slow cooker with cooking spray.

Put the pie filling, granola, water, and butter in the slow cooker and mix well. Cover and cook on LOW for 5 to 6 hours or on HIGH for 2 to 3 hours.

To serve, divide the oatmeal among 5 cereal bowls. Sprinkle each serving with extra granola for added crunch.

YIELD: 5 generous servings

ADD IT! Serve Breakfast Apple Crunch with milk or a dollop of whipped cream.

NOTE: The Golden Delicious apple is one of the best apples for cooking and baking. Interestingly enough, it's not related to the Red Delicious, which is the best apple for snacking. Other common cooking and baking apples are the Jonathan, Granny Smith, and Rome.

NUTRITIONAL ANALYSIS: One serving of the basic recipe contains 397 calories; 16 g fat; 5 g protein; 62 g carbohydrate; and 5 g dietary fiber.

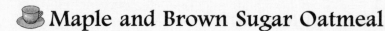 Maple and Brown Sugar Oatmeal

Cooking time: 8 to 9 hours   **Attention:** Minimal

Maple, brown sugar, and oats—what a yummy way to start the day! This recipe tastes delicious as is or served with milk.

> 5 3/4 cups (1.38 L) water
>
> 3 cups (225 g) old-fashioned **rolled oats**
>
> 1/2 cup (75 g) dark **brown sugar**, packed
>
> 1/4 teaspoon salt
>
> 3/4 teaspoon **maple flavoring**

Put the water, rolled oats, brown sugar, and salt in the slow cooker and mix well. Cover and cook on LOW for 8 to 9 hours.

Before serving, stir in the maple flavoring.

YIELD: 6 generous servings

ADD IT! Toss in 1 cup finely chopped apple or 1/2 to 1 cup chopped walnuts with the uncooked rolled oats for an extra measure of yum.

NOTE: Everyone knows that an apple a day keeps the doctor away, but did you know that walnuts are one of the most heart-healthy nuts? A 1/2 cup of walnuts contains about the same amount of omega-3 fatty acids as 3 ounces of salmon.

NUTRITIONAL ANALYSIS: One serving of the basic recipe contains 202 calories; 3 g fat; 7 g protein; 39 g carbohydrate; and 4 g dietary fiber.

 # Fruity Oatmeal

Cooking time: 8 to 9 hours	**Attention:** Minimal

Oatmeal is heart-smart, and dried fruit is loaded with antioxidants. How fitting that dried fruit tastes marvelous with oatmeal.

2 3/4 cups (660 ml) water

1 cup (75 g) old-fashioned **rolled oats**

3/4 cup (131 g) chopped mixed **dried fruit**

1 1/2 teaspoons (3.5 g) ground **cinnamon**

Put the water, rolled oats, dried fruit, and cinnamon in the slow cooker and mix well. Cover and cook on LOW for 8 to 9 hours.

Before serving, stir the oatmeal, adding more water (or milk) if a thinner consistency is desired.

YIELD: 5 generous servings

ADD IT! Sprinkle the cooked oatmeal with brown sugar or drizzle it with maple syrup for added flavor.

NOTE: In a recent study at Tufts University, dried plums ranked highest in antioxidants among all the fruits and vegetables, and raisins ranked second. You can find prepackaged bags of mixed dried fruits including these antioxidant powerhouses, plus dried apples, apricots, and a variety of other fruits, in the canned-fruit aisle of your grocery store. For this recipe, you can also buy individual bags of your favorite dried fruits and make your own combinations. Whatever you choose to do, you'll really enjoy this healthy breakfast!

NUTRITIONAL ANALYSIS: One serving of the basic recipe contains 102 calories; 1 g fat; 00 g protein; 3 g carbohydrate; and 3 g dietary fiber.

 Banana~Nut Oatmeal

Cooking time: 7 to 8 hours　　　　　　　　　**Attention:** Minimal

Try this recipe, and you'll never eat microwave oatmeal again. It's the real thing—warm, sweet, and nutty. Serve with milk or soymilk.

　1 1/2 cups (360 ml) water

　3/4 cup (56 g) old-fashioned **rolled oats**

　1/4 teaspoon salt

　2 medium **bananas**, sliced just before serving

　1/2 cup (63 g) slivered **almonds** or **chopped walnuts**

Put the water, rolled oats, and salt in the slow cooker and mix well. Cover and cook on LOW for 7 to 8 hours.

To serve, stir the oatmeal and divide it among 4 cereal bowls. Top each serving with one-fourth of the banana slices and 2 tablespoons (16 g) nuts.

YIELD: 4 servings

TIP: If the banana slices don't make the oatmeal sweet enough, add some maple syrup.

NOTE: Bananas are a staple food and an income source for developing countries. They're also the main ingredient in a popular beer made in rural eastern Africa—banana beer. A close cousin, Banana Bread Beer, won as favorite beer for women during the Great British Beer Festival in 2003.

NUTRITIONAL ANALYSIS: One serving of the basic recipe contains 219 calories; 11 g fat; 7 g protein; 27 g carbohydrate; and 4 g dietary fiber.

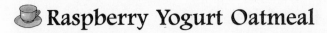Raspberry Yogurt Oatmeal

Cooking time: 7 to 8 hours **Attention:** Minimal

Getting up early for a quick morning walk or run? Have this hot but refreshing breakfast waiting when you arrive home.

1 1/2 cups (360 ml) water

3/4 cup (56 g) old-fashioned **rolled oats**

1/4 teaspoon salt

One to two 8-ounce (245-g) cartons **raspberry yogurt**

1 cup (110 g) fresh **raspberries**, washed and dried

Put the water, rolled oats, and salt in the slow cooker and mix well. Cover and cook on LOW for 7 to 8 hours.

To serve, stir the oatmeal and divide it among 4 cereal bowls. Fold one-fourth of the yogurt into each serving and top each serving with 1/2 cup of the fresh raspberries.

YIELD: 4 servings

ADD IT! Fold 2 tablespoons (16 g) slivered almonds into each serving of cooked oatmeal along with the yogurt.

NOTE: Raspberries are an excellent source of vitamin C and potassium. In addition, studies show raspberries contain a phytochemical, ellagic acid, which may help prevent cancer. They also taste pretty good.

NUTRITIONAL ANALYSIS: One serving of the basic recipe contains 144 calories; 5 g fat; 7 g protein; 19 g carbohydrate; and 4 g dietary fiber.

Honey~Nut Breakfast Rolls

The aroma of baking sweet rolls will encourage an atmosphere of ease and contentment in your home. Enjoy these rolls piping hot.

¹/₂ cup (170 g) **honey**

One 16-ounce (455-g) can refrigerator-style **buttermilk biscuits**

¹/₄ cup (31 g) chopped **pecans**, **almonds**, or **walnuts**

Coat the interior of the slow cooker's baking unit with cooking spray, and position the slow cooker's rack on the floor of the machine. If your slow cooker did not come with this equipment, use any baking pan and rack that fit inside the machine.

Put the honey in a small bowl. Dip the raw biscuits in the honey, then place them in the pan with their sides touching. Sprinkle the nuts over the raw biscuits. Place the pan in the slow cooker on the rack. Cover and cook on LOW for 3 to 4 hours; do not lift the lid during the first 2 to 3 hours.

Remove the pan from the slow cooker when it's cool enough to handle and serve the sweet rolls warm.

YIELD: 5 servings

NUTRITIONAL ANALYSIS: One serving of the basic recipe contains 478 calories; 17 g fat; 8 g protein; 77 g carbohydrate; and 3 g dietary fiber.

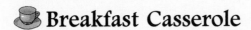 Breakfast Casserole

Cooking time: 8 to 9 hours   **Attention:** Minimal

Breakfast is the most important meal of the day. Taste this easy-to-make casserole once, and you'll never skip breakfast again. It's addictively satisfying.

>   One 1-pound (455-g) bag frozen **hash browns**, partially thawed
>
>   3 cups (338 g) **shredded cheddar** or **provolone cheese**
>
>   12 large **eggs**
>
>   1 cup (240 ml) water
>
>   1/2 teaspoon salt
>
>   1/4 teaspoon freshly ground black pepper

Spray the inside of the slow cooker with cooking spray.

Put half of the hash browns in the slow cooker and spread them out evenly. Top the hash browns with half of the cheese. Repeat with the remaining hash browns and cheese.

In a large bowl, beat the eggs with a whisk, then mix in the water, salt, and pepper. Pour the egg mixture into the slow cooker over the hash browns and cheese. Cover and cook on LOW for 8 to 9 hours.

YIELD: 8 generous servings

TIP: You don't have to thaw the hash browns unless they're rock-solid from sitting in your freezer. As long as you can sprinkle them into the slow cooker, you're good to go.

TIP: Leftover Breakfast Casserole is excellent served sandwich-style between two slices of toasted bread. Cheese lovers can add a slice of melted cheese.

ADD IT! Combine 12 ounces (120 g) bacon, cooked and crumbled, or 12 ounces (225 g) sausage, sliced and browned, with 1/2 cup sautéed chopped onion, and mix with the uncooked hash browns. For a richer casserole, substitute 1 cup milk for the water.

NUTRITIONAL ANALYSIS: One serving of the basic recipe contains 358 calories; 22 g fat; 22 g protein; 16 g carbohydrate; and 2 g dietary fiber.

Chapter 6

• •

Beverages

There's nothing like a hot drink to warm a cold winter's night. There's nothing like a hot drink to celebrate an event. There's nothing like a coffee drink to start your day. So, it's settled. Break out that slow cooker and brew up a batch of Double Blackberry Brandy-Wine (page 50), Holiday Wassail (page 49), Cinnamon-Spiked Coffee (page 54)—or whatever makes you warm, happy, and raring to go!

🏺 Spiced Apple Cider

Cooking time: 4 to 10 hours
Attention: Sample after 4 hours, then every 30 minutes

Take pleasure in the spicy aroma of this wonderful beverage as it fills your home. The drink's prettiest when served warm in tall glass mugs and garnished with apple wedges.

- 1 gallon (3.8 L) **apple cider** or **apple juice**
- 1 cup (235 ml) **cranberry juice**
- 2 **cinnamon sticks**

Pour the apple cider and cranberry juice into the slow cooker and stir to combine. Add the cinnamon sticks and stir again. Cover and heat on LOW for 4 to 10 hours, sampling the cider after 4 hours, then every 30 minutes thereafter.

When the cinnamon flavor is just right, remove the cinnamon sticks and discard them. Ladle the cider into mugs and serve it warm.

YIELD: 18 servings

ADD IT! Bundle 5 to 10 whole cloves and 2 to 3 whole allspice in a piece of cheesecloth and tie it with kitchen string. Float the bundled spices in the cider, then remove them along with the cinnamon sticks.

NUTRITIONAL ANALYSIS: One serving of the basic recipe (made with apple cider) contains 112 calories; .3 g fat; .1 g protein; 28 g carbohydrate; and .2 g dietary fiber.

🫖 Holiday Wassail

Cooking time: 4 to 6 hours
Attention: Sample after 4 hours, then every 30 minutes

Add to your joy-filled holiday gathering with this steaming–hot fruity wassail. Float a pineapple ring in the slow cooker for a festive touch.

- 1 gallon (3.8 L) **apple cider** or **apple juice**
- 2 quarts (1.9 L) unsweetened **pineapple juice**
- 2 **cinnamon sticks**

Pour the apple cider and pineapple juice into the slow cooker and stir to combine. Add the cinnamon sticks and stir again. Cover and heat on LOW for 4 to 6 hours, sampling the wassail after 4 hours, then every 30 minutes thereafter.

When the cinnamon flavor is just right, remove the cinnamon sticks and discard them.

YIELD: 24 servings

ADD IT! Add 1 cup (235 ml) strong black tea or your favorite herb tea.

NUTRITIONAL ANALYSIS: One serving of the basic recipe (made with apple cider) contains 124 calories; .3 g fat; .4 g protein; 31 g carbohydrate; and .3 g dietary fiber.

TRY THIS

Enhance the holiday feeling by serving hot wassail in vintage Santa mugs.

Double Blackberry Brandy~Wine

Cooking time: 3 to 4 hours   **Attention:** Minimal

Enjoy the unforgettable flavor of blackberries with a hint of apple. Serve very hot in small cups garnished with raisins and slivered almonds.

- 1 bottle (750 ml) **blackberry wine**
- 1 1/2 pints (710 ml) **apple juice**
- 1 cup (235 ml) **blackberry brandy** or **liqueur**

Pour the blackberry wine, apple juice, and blackberry brandy into the slow cooker and stir to combine. Cover and heat on LOW for 3 to 4 hours.

Serve the brandy-wine hot.

YIELD: 10 servings

ADD IT! For a spicy treat, add a cinnamon stick to the mixture as it's heating. Remove the cinnamon stick and discard it before serving the brandy-wine.

NUTRITIONAL ANALYSIS: One serving of the basic recipe (made with blackberry brandy) contains 125 calories; .1 g fat; .2 g protein; 15 g carbohydrate; and .1 g dietary fiber.

DID YOU KNOW?

Blackberry brandy is brandy flavored with blackberries and contains only water, alcohol, and the essential oil of the berry. Blackberry liqueur is similar to blackberry brandy, but it contains less alcohol.

Mulled Grape Cider

Cooking time: 2 to 3 hours
Attention: Sample after 1 hour, then every 30 minutes

This warm, spicy cider fills your home with the tantalizing aroma of grapes. It looks pretty when served from the slow cooker garnished with lemon and orange slices.

1 quart (.95 L) **grape juice**

2 **cinnamon sticks**

1 **lemon slice**

Put the grape juice, cinnamon sticks, and lemon slice in the slow cooker and stir to combine. Cover and heat on HIGH for 2 to 3 hours, sampling the cider after 1 hour, then every 30 minutes thereafter.

When the cinnamon flavor is just right, remove the cinnamon sticks and discard them. Remove the lemon slice or keep it as a garnish. Serve the cider warm in mugs.

YIELD: 8 servings

NUTRITIONAL ANALYSIS: One serving of the basic recipe contains 77 calories; .1 g fat; .8 g protein; 19 g carbohydrate; and .1 g dietary fiber.

🫖 Tropical Tea

Cooking time: 2 to 3 hours
Attention: Sample after 1 hour, then every 30 minutes

Enjoy a little slice of tropical paradise any day. Serve tea in a tall glass, with an orange wedge as a garnish.

2 quarts (1.9 L) boiling water

8 **black teabags**

1 1/2 pints (710 ml) **pineapple-orange juice**

1 **cinnamon stick**

Pour the boiling water into the slow cooker and add the teabags. Let the teabags steep for 5 minutes, then remove and discard them.

Add the pineapple-orange juice and cinnamon stick, and stir to combine. Cover and heat on LOW for 2 to 3 hours, sampling the tea after 1 hour, then every 30 minutes thereafter.

When the cinnamon flavor is just right, remove the cinnamon stick and discard it. Serve the tea immediately or keep it warm in the slow cooker.

YIELD: 10 servings

TIP: Substitute orange-flavored tea or herb tea for the black tea.

NUTRITIONAL ANALYSIS: One serving of the basic recipe contains 111 calories; .1 g fat; 3 g protein; 25 g carbohydrate; and .8 g dietary fiber.

🫖 Lemon-Mint Tea

Cooking time: 1 to 2 hours   **Attention:** Minimal

This blend of lemon, chamomile, and mint refreshes and soothes at the same time. It's delicious sweetened with honey.

1 1/2 quarts (1.4 L) cold water

6 **black tea with lemon-flavor teabags**

3 **chamomile teabags**

6 sprigs **fresh mint**

Pour the cold water into the slow cooker and add the teabags and fresh mint. Cover and heat on HIGH for 1 to 2 hours, or until the water begins to simmer.

Remove and discard the teabags and mint. Serve the tea immediately or keep it warm in the slow cooker.

YIELD: 6 servings

NUTRITIONAL ANALYSIS: One serving of the basic recipe contains 58 calories; 0 g fat; 3 g protein; 13 g carbohydrate; and .7 g dietary fiber.

IT'S GOOD FOR YOU

This flavorful herb tea is not only delicious, it's ideal for settling an upset stomach or as a finishing touch to a big meal.

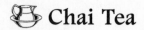 Chai Tea

Cooking time: 1 to 2 hours   **Attention:** Minimal

Traditionally served piping hot in little clay cups that are discarded after use, chai tea is fun to sip with a meal or dessert. Enjoy it with whipped cream and a sprinkle of ground cinnamon or cocoa.

  4 1/2 cups (1.1 L) cold water

  6 **chai teabags**

  1/2 cup plus 2 tablespoons (125 g) **orange** or **clover honey**

  4 1/2 cups (1.1 L) **milk**

Pour the cold water into the slow cooker and add the teabags. Cover and heat on HIGH for 1 to 2 hours, or until the water begins to simmer. Carefully remove the teabags with a slotted spoon.

Turn the slow cooker to LOW. Add the honey and stir until it has dissolved. Add the milk and stir again. Serve the tea immediately or keep it warm in the slow cooker.

YIELD: 12 servings

ADD IT! Crush a large knob of fresh ginger and add it to the cold water along with the teabags. Remove when you remove the teabags.

NUTRITIONAL ANALYSIS: One serving of the basic recipe contains 121 calories; 3 g fat; 5 g protein; 20 g carbohydrate; and .4 g dietary fiber.

 Cinnamon-Spiked Coffee

Cooking time: 2 to 3 hours
Attention: Sample after 1 hour, then every 30 minutes

Zesty coffee with a whiff of cinnamon and a whisper of brown sugar. Garnish it with whipped cream and a cinnamon stick.

  1 quart (.95 L) strong **coffee**

  1/4 cup (56 g) **brown sugar**, packed

  1 **cinnamon stick**

Put the coffee, brown sugar, and cinnamon stick in the slow cooker and stir to combine. Cover and heat on LOW for 2 to 3 hours, sampling the coffee after 1 hour, then every 30 minutes thereafter.

When the cinnamon flavor is just right, remove the cinnamon stick and discard it. Serve the coffee black or with a generous helping of half-and-half.

YIELD: 4 servings

NUTRITIONAL ANALYSIS: One serving of the basic recipe contains 57 calories; 0 g fat; .3 g protein; 14 g carbohydrate; and 0 g dietary fiber.

Raspberry Cappuccino

Cooking time: 30 to 60 minutes	**Attention:** Minimal

Perfect for a shower or bachelorette party—a raspberry-flavored explosion in a mug! It looks and tastes festive in an Irish coffee mug.

    4 $^1/_2$ cups (1.1 L) strong **coffee**

    2 cups (.47 L) **half and half**

    1 cup (.24 L) **raspberry liqueur**

Combine the ingredients into the slow cooker and mix well. Cover and heat on LOW for 30 to 60 minutes, or until the flavors have melded.

Warm 10 mugs in the oven or microwave. Divide the espresso mixture among the warm mugs, then fill the mugs the rest of the way with the prepared whipped cream. Serve the cappuccino immediately.

YIELD: 10 servings

ADD IT! Top the whipped cream with chocolate curls, dust it with ground cinnamon or cocoa powder, or drizzle it with raspberry sauce.

NUTRITIONAL ANALYSIS: One serving of the basic recipe contains 101 calories; 6 g fat; 2 g protein; 11 g carbohydrate; and 0 g dietary fiber.

🫖 Café Mocha

Cooking time: 2 to 3 hours

Attention: Stir occasionally; watch to keep from simmering

For an event or just to savor the day with your sweetheart, enjoy this chocolaty taste treat along with Belgian chocolates, Cinnamon Walnuts (page 75), or fresh strawberries dipped in dark chocolate.

> 5 cups (1.2 L) strong **coffee**
>
> Five to six 1-ounce (28-g) envelopes **hot chocolate mix**
>
> Prepared **whipped cream**

Put the coffee and hot chocolate mix in the slow cooker and stir until the hot chocolate mix has completely dissolved. Cover and heat on LOW for 2 to 3 hours, or until the mixture is hot, stirring occasionally; do not let it simmer.

Serve the coffee in mugs, topped with dollops of the whipped cream.

YIELD: 6 servings

ADD IT! Dust the whipped cream with ground cinnamon or cocoa powder.

NUTRITIONAL ANALYSIS: One serving of the basic recipe (made with 5 envelopes hot chocolate mix and without whipped cream) contains 86 calories; .7 g fat; 1 g protein; 22 g carbohydrate; and 1 g dietary fiber.

IT'S GOOD FOR YOU

Chocolate's health benefits have been making headlines. It's now being touted as a preventive for everything from heart disease to cancer—consumed in moderation, of course! So be good to your heart and your sweetheart, and serve up this rich chocolate concoction.

🍵 Peppermint Hot Cocoa

Cooking time: 2 to 3 hours

Attention: Add more ingredients after 30 minutes; watch to keep from simmering

This recipe is great for large groups.

    1 gallon (3.8 L) cold **milk**
    1 to 2 cups (235 to 470 ml) **chocolate-flavored syrup**
    1/2 to 1 cup (120 to 235 ml) **peppermint-flavored syrup**

Pour the cold milk into the slow cooker. Cover and heat on LOW for 30 minutes, or until the milk is warm enough to dissolve the syrups.

Add the chocolate- and peppermint-flavored syrups and gently stir until the syrups have dissolved. Cover and continue heating on LOW for another 1 1/2 to 2 1/2 hours, or until the mixture is hot; do not let it simmer.

Serve the cocoa warm in mugs topped with whipped cream and crushed mint candies.

YIELD: 18 servings

NUTRITIONAL ANALYSIS: One serving of the basic recipe (made with 1 cup chocolate-flavored syrup and 1/2 cup peppermint-flavored syrup) contains 188 calories; 7 g fat; 8 g protein; 25 g carbohydrate; and .4 g dietary fiber.

TRY THIS

Instead of peppermint, try substituting raspberry or hazelnut syrup.

☕ Coquito Eggnog

Cooking time: 1 to 2 hours

Attention: Watch to keep from simmering

It's good to create a new holiday tradition. Chilled coconut eggnog is a delicious tradition in Puerto Rico. Try it and see why.

    2 quarts (1.9 L) **eggnog**
    1 pint (475 ml) **coconut milk**
    1/2 teaspoon ground **nutmeg**

Pour the eggnog and coconut milk into the slow cooker and stir gently to combine. Cover and heat on LOW for 1 to 2 hours, or until the mixture is hot; do not let it simmer.

Ladle the eggnog into mugs, dust it with nutmeg, and serve it warm. To be traditional, refrigerate it for several hours and serve it chilled.

YIELD: 10 servings

NUTRITIONAL ANALYSIS: One serving of the basic recipe contains 383 calories; 27 g fat; 9 g protein; 30 g carbohydrate; and 1 g dietary fiber.

IT'S GOOD FOR YOU

There's more to coconuts than the milk and those shreds you use in baking. Coconut oil has been touted as the new weight-loss miracle food! Try cooking with coconut oil instead of your current cooking oil—unlike coconut milk and flesh, the oil won't add a coconut flavor to your food.

Chapter 7

• •

Dips and Appetizers

Simplify, simplify, simplify. That's the mantra. It has a romantic appeal at first blush, but what does it really mean? Related to good eats, it can mean taking out a slow cooker or two for your next party. With a slow cooker, you can prepare and cook an appetizer or dip quickly, plus keep it warm while serving it! No need for chafing dishes, warming trays, fuel for heating, matches, or a lighter. Better yet, simplify dinner—serve a hearty appetizer as the main course!

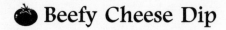 Beefy Cheese Dip

Cooking time: 30 to 60 minutes   **Attention:** Minimal

Prepare this dish with mild or spicy tomatoes—it's up to you. Serve it with tortilla chips and a side of guacamole on shredded lettuce.

Two 16-ounce (455-g) jars double **cheddar cheese sauce**

1 pound (455 g) **ground beef**, browned and drained

One 10-ounce (280-g) can **diced tomatoes with green chiles**, undrained

Put the cheese sauce, browned ground beef, and diced tomatoes in the slow cooker and stir to combine. Cover and cook on LOW for 30 to 60 minutes, or until the mixture is hot and the cheese has melted.

Stir the dip and serve it immediately, or keep it warm in the slow cooker.

YIELD: 12 appetizer servings

NUTRITIONAL ANALYSIS: One serving of the basic recipe contains 195 calories; 14 g fat; 10 g protein; 7 g carbohydrate; and .7 g dietary fiber.

TRY THIS

Next time you're in a festive mood, call up some friends, whip up this dip and a batch of margaritas, put a favorite movie on, and kick back.

● Chili con Queso Dip

Cooking time: 3 to 3 1/2 hours
Attention: Remove cover during final hour

Always the first to go at parties, this dip is wonderful with tortilla chips or with warm flour tortillas torn into bite-size pieces. The recipe is easily doubled.

1 1/2 pounds (683 g) pasteurized **processed cheese food**, Mexican-flavored or plain, cut into cubes

One 19-ounce (540-g) can **chunky-style chili**, with or without beans

1/2 cup (30 g) chopped fresh **cilantro**

Salt and freshly ground black pepper

Put the cheese food, chili, and cilantro in the slow cooker and stir to combine. Season with salt and pepper to taste and stir again. Cover and cook on LOW for 2 to 2 1/2 hours, or until the cheese has melted, stirring occasionally.

Uncover and cook for 1 more hour, or until the mixture is hot.

Stir the dip and serve it immediately, or keep it warm in the slow cooker.

YIELD: 12 appetizer servings

ADD IT! Garnish the dip with shredded cheddar cheese, chopped tomato, a dollop of sour cream, or chopped green onion for added visual appeal.

NUTRITIONAL ANALYSIS: One serving of the basic recipe (made with chili without beans) contains 339 calories; 23 g fat; 22 g protein; 16 g carbohydrate; and 1 g dietary fiber.

 Sausage Nacho Dip

Cooking time: 2 1/2 to 3 1/2 hours	**Attention:** Stir occasionally

Sausage, cheese, and salsa combine for a marvelous dip to go with tortilla chips, soft tortilla triangles, or sourdough bread cubes. Sit back and watch it disappear.

1 pound (455 g) bulk garlic **sausage**, browned and drained

1 pound (455 g) pasteurized **processed cheese food**, Mexican-flavored or plain, cut into cubes

One 16-ounce (455 g) jar mild or medium-hot chunky-style **salsa**

Salt and freshly ground black pepper

Put the browned sausage, cheese food, and salsa in the slow cooker and stir to combine. Cover and cook on LOW for 2 1/2 to 3 1/2 hours, or until the cheese has melted and the mixture is hot, stirring occasionally.

Season the dip with salt and pepper to taste and stir it again. Serve the dip warm from the slow cooker.

YIELD: 12 appetizer servings

TIP: If you don't have sausage on hand, replace it with 1 pound (455 g) ground beef, browned and drained, combined with 1 small onion, chopped and sautéed.

NUTRITIONAL ANALYSIS: One serving of the basic recipe contains 358 calories; 30 g fat; 17 g protein; 10 g carbohydrate; and .6 g dietary fiber.

🍅 Pepper Jack~Chicken Dip

Cooking time: 2 to 3 hours	**Attention:** Minimal

The zesty cheese makes this change-of-pace dip a crowd pleaser. Serve with white tortilla chips or French bread cubes.

One 10³/4-ounce (305-g) can condensed **cream of chicken soup**

One 10-ounce (280-g) can **chicken breast**, drained

8 ounces (225 g) hot **pepper jack cheese**, shredded

Salt and freshly ground black pepper

Put the condensed soup, chicken breast, and cheese in the slow cooker and stir to combine. Season with salt and pepper to taste and stir the mixture again. Cover and cook on LOW for 2 to 3 hours.

Stir the dip and serve it immediately, or keep it warm in the slow cooker.

YIELD: 8 appetizer servings

ADD IT! Add 1/4 to 1/2 teaspoon crushed red pepper along with the salt and black pepper to spice up the dip even more.

NUTRITIONAL ANALYSIS: One serving of the basic recipe contains 194 calories; 13 g fat; 16 g protein; 3 g carbohydrate; and .1 g dietary fiber.

TRY THIS

If you're not a hot-pepper fan but still want a dip that packs a flavor punch, substitute extra-sharp white cheddar cheese for the pepper jack.

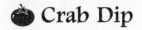 Crab Dip

Cooking time: 2 to 4 hours   **Attention:** Minimal

Easy to make and oh-so-flavorful. Serve this dip in an edible bread bowl or with assorted crackers, raw vegetables, or blue corn chips.

> One 8-ounce (225-g) package **cream cheese**, softened
>
> 1 scant cup (225 g) **mayonnaise**
>
> 1 pound (455 g) lump **crabmeat**, drained and cartilage removed

Put the softened cream cheese in a medium-size bowl. Add mayonnaise to taste and stir to combine. Transfer the mixture to the slow cooker. Add the crabmeat and gently stir, being careful not to shred the lumps. Cover and cook on LOW for 2 to 4 hours.

Stir the dip and serve it immediately, or keep it warm in the slow cooker for up to 2 hours.

YIELD: 8 appetizer servings

ADD IT! Add 1 onion, finely minced, to the mayonnaise and cream cheese mixture. Add $1/2$ teaspoon Old Bay Seafood Seasoning for a special treat.

NUTRITIONAL ANALYSIS: One serving of the basic recipe contains 352 calories; 34 g fat; 14 g protein; .8 g carbohydrate; and 0 g dietary fiber.

TRY THIS

Serve this decadent dip with an ice-cold glass of rose, sweet, or dry wine as you and your guests prefer. Great with icy mugs of beer, too!

Broccoli and Cheese Dip

Cooking time: 3 to 4 hours

Attention: Stir occasionally during first 30 minutes; add more ingredients after 30 minutes

Enjoy how simple and easy it is to make this popular dip. Delicious with tortilla chips, crackers, and bread chunks.

> 1 pound (455 g) pasteurized **processed cheese food**, cut into cubes
>
> One 16-ounce (455-g) bag frozen **broccoli florets**, partially thawed
>
> One 10^3/4-ounce (305-g) can condensed **cream of broccoli soup**
>
> Salt

Put the cheese food in the slow cooker. Cover and heat on LOW for 30 minutes, or until the cheese has melted, stirring occasionally.

In a medium-size bowl, combine the broccoli florets and condensed soup. Add the broccoli-soup mixture to the melted cheese in the slow cooker and stir to blend. Season the mixture with salt to taste and stir it again. Cover and cook on LOW for 2 ^{1}/2 to 3 ^{1}/2 hours, or until the mixture is hot.

Stir the dip and serve it immediately, or keep it warm in the slow cooker.

YIELD: 10 appetizer servings

ADD IT! Add 2 cloves garlic, minced, to the melted cheese. For a creamier dip, stir in ^{1}/2 cup (115 g) sour cream right before serving.

NUTRITIONAL ANALYSIS: One serving of the basic recipe contains 258 calories; 18 g fat; 16 g protein; 13 g carbohydrate; and 2 g dietary fiber.

🍅 White Cheese~Mushroom Dip

Cooking time: 1 1/2 to 2 1/2 hours	**Attention:** Stir occasionally

A tasty twist on the usual white-cheese dip. Serve with breadsticks or whole-wheat crackers.

> 4 cups (452 g) shredded **asadero cheese**
>
> 1 cup (235 ml) **milk** or **half-and-half**
>
> One 4-ounce (115-g) can marinated sliced **mushrooms**
>
> Salt

Put the asadero cheese, milk, and mushrooms in the slow cooker and stir to combine. Season the mixture with salt to taste and stir it again. Cover and cook on LOW for 1 1/2 to 2 1/2 hours, or until the cheese has melted, stirring occasionally.

Stir the dip and serve it hot from the slow cooker, accompanied by breadsticks or crackers.

YIELD: 18 appetizer servings

NUTRITIONAL ANALYSIS: One serving of the basic recipe (made with milk) contains 102 calories; 8 g fat; 6 g protein; 1 g carbohydrate; and .2 g dietary fiber.

WATCH THIS

Make sure the cheese you choose is true asadero, not Muenster with the rind removed. This type of Mexican cheese, also called Chihuahua or Oaxaca cheese, melts without separating into oil and solids. This makes it perfect for slow-cooker dips. You can find it at the supermarket in balls, braids, or rounds.

 Pizza Dip

Cooking time: 30 to 60 minutes   **Attention:** Minimal

All your favorite pizza flavors in a dip. Yummy with tortilla chips, chunks of Italian bread, and breadsticks.

> One 8-ounce (225-g) package **cream cheese**, softened
>
> One 14-ounce (398-g) jar **pizza sauce**
>
> 2 cups (224 g) shredded pizza-blend **cheese**

Spread the softened cream cheese in the bottom of the slow cooker. Pour the pizza sauce over the cream cheese, then sprinkle the cheese over the sauce. Cover and cook on LOW for 30 to 60 minutes, or until the cheese has melted.

Stir the dip and serve it immediately, or keep it warm in the slow cooker.

YIELD: 10 appetizer servings

ADD IT! Add 2 to 4 ounces (55 to 115 g) pepperoni, sliced and quartered, to the pizza sauce before adding it to the slow cooker.

NUTRITIONAL ANALYSIS: One serving of the basic recipe contains 178 calories; 15 g fat; 7 g protein; 5 g carbohydrate; and 0 g dietary fiber.

TRY THIS

For extra decadence, serve this scrumptious dip with pizza breadsticks.

🍅 Chili~Cheese Dip

Cooking time 3 to 3 1/2 hours
Attention: Stir occasionally; remove cover during final hour

A hot dip with a bit of a bite, sure to heat up any party. If you want to kick it up a notch, add a splash of hot sauce.

1 pound (455 g) pasteurized **processed cheese food**, Mexican-flavored or plain, cut into cubes

One 12-ounce (340-g) jar hot chunky-style **salsa**

One 4-ounce (115-g) can chopped **green chile peppers**, drained

Salt and freshly ground black pepper

Put the cheese food, salsa, and green chiles in the slow cooker and stir to combine. Season the mixture with salt and pepper to taste and stir it again. Cover and cook on LOW for 2 to 2 1/2 hours, or until the cheese has melted, stirring occasionally.

Uncover and cook for 1 more hour, or until the mixture is hot.

Stir the dip and serve it immediately, or keep it warm in the slow cooker.

YIELD: 8 appetizer servings

ADD IT! Garnish the dip with shredded cheddar cheese, chopped tomato, a dollop of sour cream, or chopped green onion for added visual appeal. Serve with tortilla chips or warm flour tortillas torn into bite-size pieces.

NUTRITIONAL ANALYSIS: One serving of the basic recipe contains 300 calories; 21 g fat; 19 g protein; 14 g carbohydrate; and .9 g dietary fiber.

🍅 Party Meatballs

Cooking time: 3 1/2 to 4 1/2 hours on LOW   1 1/2 to 2 1/2 hours on HIGH
Attention: Minimal

Variety is the spice of life. At your next party, treat your guests to this tasty twist on an old favorite—sweet-and-spicy meatballs.

1 1/2 cups (480 g) **raspberry jelly**

1/2 cup (169 g) **chili sauce**

One 1-pound (455-g) bag frozen fully cooked **meatballs**, completely thawed

Put the raspberry jelly and chili sauce in the slow cooker and stir to combine. Add the meatballs and stir to coat them with the sauce. Cover and cook on LOW for 3 1/2 to 4 1/2 hours or on HIGH for 1 1/2 to 2 1/2 hours, or until the mixture is hot.

Before serving, stir the meatballs to coat them with sauce again.

YIELD: 6 appetizer servings

TIP: This recipe can be easily doubled for big crowds.

NUTRITIONAL ANALYSIS: One serving of the basic recipe contains 444 calories; 20 g fat; 10 g protein; 61 g carbohydrate; and 3 g dietary fiber.

🍅 Cranberry Meatballs

Cooking time: 3 to 4 hours	**Attention:** Minimal

The cranberries make this appetizer great for holiday parties. It's tasty enough for the rest of the year, too.

> One 16-ounce (455-g) can whole-berry or jellied **cranberry sauce**
>
> 3/4 cup (169) **chili sauce**
>
> 1/4 cup (60 ml) water
>
> Two 1-pound (455-g) bags frozen fully cooked **meatballs**, completely thawed

Put the cranberry sauce, chili sauce, and water in the slow cooker and stir to combine. Add the meatballs and stir to coat them with the sauce. Cover and cook on LOW for 3 to 4 hours.

Stir the meatballs again, and serve them warm from the slow cooker.

YIELD: 8 servings

ADD IT! Add 2 packed tablespoons (28 g) brown sugar and 1 teaspoon lemon juice to the sauce.

NUTRITIONAL ANALYSIS: One serving of the basic recipe contains 439 calories; 30 g fat; 15 g protein; 31 g carbohydrate; and 4 g dietary fiber.

🍅 Apple~Maple~Kielbasa Appetizer

Cooking time: 6 to 8 hours   **Attention:** Minimal

Maple, applesauce, and sausage blend to perfection in this kielbasa appetizer. Serve with fancy toothpicks and cute cocktail napkins.

  2 pounds (910 g) fully cooked Polska kielbasa **sausage**, sliced into 1/2-inch (1.3-cm) coins

  One 16-ounce (455-g) jar natural **applesauce**

  3/4 cup (242 g) pure **maple syrup**

In a large skillet over medium heat, brown the sausage coins to render out the fat. Drain the coins between several layers of paper toweling.

Put the applesauce and maple syrup in the slow cooker and stir to combine. Add the sausage coins and stir to coat them with the sauce. Cover and cook on LOW for 6 to 8 hours, or until the mixture is hot.

YIELD: 12 appetizer servings

NUTRITIONAL ANALYSIS: One serving of the basic recipe contains 302 calories; 21 g fat; 10 g protein; 19 g carbohydrate; and .4 g dietary fiber.

IT'S GOOD FOR YOU

Pure maple syrup is not just a delightful sweetener, extracted from the sap of sugar maple trees, which flow amber sap into buckets for up to a century. Maple syrup contains fewer calories than honey and is more nutritious. It's a decent source of calcium, iron, and the B vitamin thiamin. That's logical, really, as it takes up to 50 gallons (189 L) of sap to produce 1 gallon (3.78 L) of syrup.

 Fruit Chutney

Consider making your Fruit Chutney separate from the holiday ham. Your vegetarian friends and relatives will love you for it.

> One 12-ounce (340-g) jar fruit **chutney**
>
> 1 cup (175 g) chopped mixed **dried fruit with raisins**
>
> 1 tablespoon (14 ml) raspberry **balsamic vinegar**

Put the fruit chutney, mixed dried fruit with raisins, and balsamic vinegar in the slow cooker and stir to combine. Cover and cook on LOW for 6 to 8 hours, or until the flavors have melded.

Turn the heat OFF and allow the chutney to cool, then transfer the chutney to a covered bowl and store it in the refrigerator. Serve it at room temperature.

YIELD: 6 servings

NUTRITIONAL ANALYSIS: One serving of the basic recipe contains 181 calories; .3 g fat; .5 g protein; 46 g carbohydrate; and 3 g dietary fiber.

TRY THIS

Make Ham and Fruit Chutney. Put a fully cooked ham in the slow cooker, then combine all the other ingredients in a separate bowl and pour them over the ham. Cover and cook on LOW for 6 to 8 hours.

🍅 Apple Butter

Cooking time: 10 to 11 hours

Attention: Stir once an hour; mash apples and add another ingredient after 4¹/₂ to 5 hours

What's cooking for breakfast? Serve Apple Butter on your favorite breakfast bread, pancakes, or waffles, or with apple or pear wedges.

- 14 medium **cooking apples** (such as Jonathan, Granny Smith, or Rome), peeled or unpeeled, cored, and sliced
- 1 cup (235 ml) **apple juice**
- 2 ¹/₂ cups (473 g) **Cinnamon Sugar** (page 29)

Sterilize 2 glass jars with tight-fitting lids and set them aside. Spray the inside of the slow cooker with cooking spray.

Put the apples and apple juice in the slow cooker. Cover and cook on HIGH for 4 ¹/₂ to 5 hours, or until the apples are tender, stirring once an hour.

Turn the heat OFF and allow the slow cooker to cool enough so that you can handle the ceramic pot safely. Mash the apples with a fork until they're fairly smooth. If desired, strain them to remove the peels or pulse them in small batches in a blender or food processor, then return them to the slow cooker. Add the Cinnamon Sugar and stir to combine. Cover and cook on HIGH for another 5 ¹/₂ to 6 hours, stirring at least once an hour.

Once the apple butter has become thick and spreadable, turn the slow cooker OFF. Cool the apple butter to room temperature. Ladle the apple butter into the prepared jars and screw on the lids. Store the apple butter in the refrigerator.

YIELD: 16 servings

ADD IT! Add ¹/₄ teaspoon ground cloves and/or ¹/₂ teaspoon ground ginger along with the Cinnamon Sugar for a spicier apple-butter flavor.

NUTRITIONAL ANALYSIS: One serving of the basic recipe contains 192 calories; 5 g fat; .3 g protein; 50 g carbohydrate; and 5 g dietary fiber.

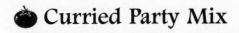 Curried Party Mix

Cooking time: 4 to 6 hours

Attention: Stir every 30 minutes; change heat setting after 30 minutes

Soothe the crunchy munchies with this spicy party mix. Enjoy with plenty of your favorite beverage.

- 3 tablespoons (42 g) **butter**, melted
- 1 teaspoon (2 g) **curry powder**
- 7 cups (343 g) bite-size **square cereal**, rice, corn, and/or oat flavors

Put the melted butter and curry powder in the slow cooker and stir to combine. Add the cereal and stir until the pieces are evenly coated. Cook uncovered on HIGH for 2 hours, stirring every 30 minutes.

Reduce the heat to LOW and cook for an additional 2 to 4 hours, or until the cereal becomes a golden color.

Line a baking sheet with several layers of paper toweling. Transfer the party mix to the baking sheet and allow it to cool.

When the party mix has completely cooled, serve it immediately or pour it into an airtight container for storage.

YIELD: 28 appetizer servings

ADD IT! Increase the butter to 4 tablespoons (55 g), and add 1 cup (150 g) shelled mixed nuts and 1 cup (227 g) pretzel sticks along with the cereal. Increase the curry powder to taste. Lightly sprinkle the party mix with 1 teaspoon salt while it's cooling on the baking sheet.

NUTRITIONAL ANALYSIS: One serving of the basic recipe contains 61 calories; 2 g fat; 1 g protein; 12 g carbohydrate; and 2 g dietary fiber.

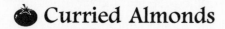 Curried Almonds

Cooking time: 3 1/2 to 5 hours
Attention: Change heat setting and uncover after 2 to 3 hours

Are you a party nut? Or do you just like serving them? Curried Almonds are a crunchy addition to chicken salad, curried rice, or your party table.

- 8 tablespoons (1 stick, or 112 g) **butter**, melted
- 1 tablespoon (6 g) **curry powder**
- 1 teaspoon salt
- 8 cups (2 pounds, or 910 g) blanched whole **almonds**

Put the melted butter, curry powder, and salt in the slow cooker and stir to combine. Add the almonds and stir until they're evenly coated. Cover and cook on LOW for 2 to 3 hours.

Raise the heat to HIGH, remove the cover, and cook the mixture for another 1 1/2 to 2 hours, stirring occasionally.

YIELD: 32 servings

NOTE: Almonds have almost as much calcium as milk. If that isn't enough to drive you to the store for a bag o' nuts, almonds are also high in the antioxidants selenium and vitamin E.

NUTRITIONAL ANALYSIS: One serving of the basic recipe contains 235 calories; 21 g fat; 7 g protein; 7 g carbohydrate; and 4 g dietary fiber.

Cajun Pecans

Cooking time: 1 1/2 to 2 1/2 hours
Attention: Change heat setting and remove cover after 15 minutes; stir occasionally

Try a spicy treat that's a little different—Cajun Pecans. It's a healthy snack with a kick.

- 4 tablespoons (55 g) **butter**, melted
- 1 teaspoon **Cajun seasoning**
- 4 cups (1 pound, or 455 g) **pecan halves**

Put the melted butter and Cajun seasoning in the slow cooker and stir to combine. Add the pecan halves and stir until they're evenly coated. Cover and cook on HIGH for 15 minutes.

Reduce the heat to LOW and cook uncovered for an additional 1 1/2 to 2 hours, stirring occasionally.

YIELD: 16 servings

TIP: Pack these pecans into decorative glass jars for holiday gift-giving.

ADD IT! Add a splash of hot sauce—as much as you dare—to the melted butter for an extra hot Cajun taste.

NUTRITIONAL ANALYSIS: One serving of the basic recipe contains 206 calories; 21 g fat; 2 g protein; 5 g carbohydrate; and 2 g dietary fiber.

🍅 Cinnamon Walnuts

Cooking time: 1 1/2 to 2 1/2 hours
Attention: Change heat setting and remove cover after 15 minutes; stir occasionally

These exquisite nuts are the perfect complement to fresh peaches, pears, apples, and strawberries. Good together, and good for you.

4 cups (1 pound, or 455 g) **walnut halves**

8 tablespoons (1 stick, or 112 g) **butter**, melted

1/2 cup (95 g) **Cinnamon Sugar** (page 29)

Put the walnut haves and melted butter in the slow cooker and mix well. Add the Cinnamon Sugar and stir until the walnut halves are evenly coated. Cover and cook on HIGH for 15 minutes.

Reduce the heat to LOW and cook uncovered for another 1 1/2 to 2 hours, or until the nuts are coated with a glaze, stirring occasionally.

Transfer the walnuts to a bowl and allow them to cool completely.

YIELD: 16 appetizer servings

ADD IT! When the walnuts are done but still in the slow cooker, sprinkle them with 1/2 teaspoon apple pie spice and stir to coat them evenly.

NUTRITIONAL ANALYSIS: One serving of the basic recipe contains 263 calories; 23 g fat; 8 g protein; 10 g carbohydrate; and 2 g dietary fiber.

🍅 Hot and Spicy Nuts

Cooking time: 2 1/2 to 3 1/2 hours
Attention: Change heat setting and remove cover after 20 to 25 minutes; stir occasionally

Will you make these specialty nuts mild, scalding, or somewhere in between? Any way you serve them, make sure your guests have a cooling beverage accompaniment.

5 1/2 tablespoons (1/3 cup, or 75 g) **butter**, melted

2 teaspoons (6 g) mild or spicy **Mexican seasoning**

1 1/2 cups (150 g) shelled whole **pecans** or **walnut halves**

Salt

Put the melted butter and Mexican seasoning in the slow cooker and stir to combine. Add the nuts and stir until they're evenly coated. Cover and cook on HIGH for 20 to 25 minutes.

Reduce the heat to LOW and cook uncovered for an additional 2 to 3 hours, stirring occasionally.

Transfer the nuts to a baking sheet and allow them to cool. Sprinkle them with salt to taste. Serve them warm or at room temperature.

YIELD: 12 servings

ADD IT! Add 1/2 teaspoon onion or garlic powder along with the Mexican seasoning, or use onion or garlic salt in place of the plain salt.

NUTRITIONAL ANALYSIS: One serving of the basic recipe (made with shelled whole pecans) contains 137 calories; 14 g fat; 1 g protein; 3 g carbohydrate; and 1 g dietary fiber.

Chapter 8

• •

Soups

Nurturing, soothing, and satisfying—soup is a comfort food that's been feeding the human soul for centuries. More often than not, we eat comfort foods when we're happy, relaxed, and in a mood to reward ourselves. We feel good about choosing healthful foods such as soups that pass the "Mom test"— foods that bring back happy memories of mom's cooking and nurturing care. A steaming bowl of healthful soup is quite a reward to your palate, especially when it's so easy to fix in the slow cooker. Try our Beef-Barley Soup (page 78), Chicken-Dumpling Soup (page 81), or Creamy Potato Soup (page 88) to start.

🍲 Beef-Barley Soup

Cooking time: 5 to 6 hours   **Attention:** Minimal

Beef, barley, and vegetables combine for a soup sensation that can't be beat. Serve in large bowls, and accompany with a green salad and crusty bread.

    2 quarts (1.9 L) water

    One 9-ounce (255-g) package vegetable-barley **soup mix**

    2 pounds (910 g) **beef chuck roast,** cut into cubes

    1 small **onion,** chopped

    Salt and freshly ground black pepper

Put the water and soup mix in the slow cooker and stir until the soup mix has dissolved. Add the beef cubes and chopped onion, season the mixture with salt and pepper to taste, and stir again. Cover and cook on LOW for 5 to 6 hours.

YIELD: 10 servings

NUTRITIONAL ANALYSIS: One serving of the basic recipe contains 263 calories; 16 g fat; 16 g protein; 14 g carbohydrate; and 1 g dietary fiber.

TRY THIS

To clean your slow cooker, pour soapy water (about the same strength as you use to hand-wash dishes) inside your slow cooker and let it cook on high for at least an hour before rinsing. One more proof that slow cooking is super-convenient!

Steak, Onion, and Mushroom Noodle Soup

Cooking time: 8 1/2 to 11 hours
Attention: Change heat setting and add another ingredient during final 30 to 60 minutes

Rich, fall-apart-tender chunks of beef taste mouth-wateringly delicious in an onion-mushroom broth. Ladle into soup bowls and serve with a grilled cheddar cheese sandwich.

5 1/2 cups (1.3 L) water

Two 1.8-ounce (50-g) envelopes **onion-mushroom soup mix**

1 pound (455 g) **round steak**, cut into small pieces

8 ounces (225 g) dry **egg noodles**

Salt and freshly ground black pepper

Put the water and soup mix in the slow cooker and stir until the soup mix has dissolved. Add the steak pieces and stir again. Cover and cook on LOW for 8 to 10 hours.

Raise the heat to HIGH and add the egg noodles. Cover and cook for another 30 to 60 minutes, or until the egg noodles are tender and the soup has thickened.

Before serving, stir the soup and season it with salt and pepper to taste.

YIELD: 8 generous servings

NUTRITIONAL ANALYSIS: One serving of the basic recipe contains 237 calories; 9 g fat; 15 g protein; 24 g carbohydrate; and 1 g dietary fiber.

Italian Meatball Soup

This soup couldn't be easier to make. Just drop the ingredients in the slow cooker, and you'll find a tasty soup waiting for you when you return from your long day.

- 1 quart (.95 L) hot water
- 6 beef **bouillon cubes**
- Two 14-ounce (398-g) cans **diced tomatoes** with garlic, undrained
- 1-pound (455-g) bag frozen fully cooked Italian-style **meatballs**, completely thawed

Put the hot water and bouillon cubes in the slow cooker and stir until the bouillon cubes have dissolved. Add the diced tomatoes and meatballs, and stir again. Cover and cook on LOW for 6 to 8 hours.

YIELD: 10 servings

ADD IT! Add a 16-ounce (455-g) bag frozen mixed vegetables, thawed, along with the diced tomatoes and meatballs.

NUTRITIONAL ANALYSIS: One serving of the basic recipe contains 161 calories; 12 g fat; 7 g protein; 7 g carbohydrate; and 2 g dietary fiber.

TRY THIS

Crusty Italian bread, a crisp green salad, and a glass of Chianti makes this a perfect week-day meal.

Chicken-Dumpling Soup

Cooking time: 2 to 3 hours

Attention: Change heat setting and prepare and add another ingredient during final 30 to 60 minutes

This soup is absolutely delicious and oh-so-simple to make. A true one-pot meal.

Three 19-ounce (540-g) cans ready-to-eat chunky **chicken noodle soup**

1 cup (120 g) all-purpose **buttermilk baking mix**

5 to 6 tablespoons (75 to 90 ml) **milk**

Put the chicken noodle soup in the slow cooker, cover, and cook on LOW for 1 to 1 1/2 hours, or until the soup is very hot.

Raise the heat to HIGH. When the soup begins to simmer (in about 20 minutes), and not before, put the baking mix and milk in a medium-size bowl and stir just until the baking mix is moistened; do not overmix or the dumplings will be tough. Uncover the slow cooker and, using a tablespoon, drop the dough by spoonfuls into the hot soup; leave space around each dumpling, since the dumplings will expand and merge as they cook. Cover and cook for another 30 to 60 minutes, or until the dumplings are done; do not lift the lid or the dumplings will not finish cooking.

YIELD: 6 generous servings

NUTRITIONAL ANALYSIS: One serving of the basic recipe (made with 5 tablespoons milk) contains 171 calories; 6 g fat; 6 g protein; 24 g carbohydrate; and .8 g dietary fiber.

SPEED IT UP

For faster-to-the-table Chicken-Dumpling Soup, preheat the canned chicken noodle soup in a microwave-safe bowl according to the soup-label directions. Carefully ladle the hot soup into the slow cooker and turn the heat to HIGH, then begin preparing the dumplings. You'll have an extra dish to wash, but you'll save yourself 1 to 1 1/2 hours in heating time.

Grandma's Turkey Noodle Soup

Cooking time: 10 1/2 to 12 1/2 hours
Attention: Change heat setting, strain broth, debone meat, and add more ingredients during final 15 to 30 minutes

A tasty and healthful way to use up leftover turkey and stuffing after the holidays.

> 1 1/2 quarts (1.4 L) hot water
>
> 6 chicken **bouillon cubes**
>
> 2 to 3 pounds (.9 to 1.4 kg) leftover **turkey**, including meat, skin, bones, and stuffing
>
> Salt and freshly ground black pepper
>
> 1 cup (160 g) fresh or frozen **egg noodles**

Put the hot water and bouillon cubes in the slow cooker and stir until the bouillon cubes have dissolved. Add the turkey meat, skin, bones, and stuffing, and stir again. Cover and cook on LOW for 10 to 12 hours.

Turn the heat OFF and allow the slow cooker to cool enough so that you can handle the ceramic pot safely. Transfer the contents of the slow cooker to a large bowl, then strain off the broth and return it to the ceramic pot. Remove the turkey meat from the bones, chop it into bite-size pieces, and return it to the slow cooker. Stir the mixture and season it with salt and pepper to taste. Turn the heat to HIGH, stir in the egg noodles, and cook for another 15 to 30 minutes, or until the noodles are tender.

YIELD: 8 servings

ADD IT! Add 1 1/2 cups (340 g) frozen Seasoning-Blend Vegetables (page 30) and 2 to 3 fresh broccoli stalks (without the florets) along with the turkey meat, skin, bones, and stuffing for a more flavorful broth.

NUTRITIONAL ANALYSIS: One serving of the basic recipe (made with 2 pounds turkey meat) contains 170 calories; 8 g fat; 83 g protein; 4 g carbohydrate; and .1 g dietary fiber.

🏺 Spicy Clam Chowder

Cooking time: 2 to 3 hours

Attention: Change heat setting and add another ingredient during final 30 minutes; watch to keep from boiling

The rich taste of this clam chowder provides the ultimate in satisfaction. Hot, buttered cornbread is a delicious and traditional accompaniment.

Three 19-ounce (540-g) cans ready-to-eat chunky **potato soup**

One 10-ounce (280-g) can **baby clams**, drained, with 1/2 cup (60 ml) juice reserved

1/2 teaspoon **Old Bay Seafood Seasoning**

Salt and freshly ground black pepper

Put the potato soup, reserved clam juice, and Old Bay Seafood Seasoning in the slow cooker and stir to combine. Cover and cook on LOW for 1 1/2 to 2 1/2 hours.

Add the clams and cook the soup for another 30 minutes, or until the clams are hot. To hasten the warming of the clams, raise the heat to HIGH, but do not allow the soup to boil or the clams will become tough.

Before serving, stir the soup and season it with salt and pepper to taste.

YIELD: 6 generous servings

ADD IT! For a richer chowder, add 4 tablespoons (55 g) butter, melted, along with the salt and pepper. Garnish each serving with crumbled bacon.

NUTRITIONAL ANALYSIS: One serving of the basic recipe contains 162 calories; 4 g fat; 17 g protein; 15 g carbohydrate; and 1 g dietary fiber.

DID YOU KNOW?

The original slow cooker, the Rival Crock Pot, was introduced in 1971. It was developed from a baked-bean cooker called The Beanery. To date, over 100 million Crock Pots have been sold! A host of sophisticated slow cookers have come on the market in recent years from Rival and other companies like Hamilton Beach, Cuisinart, Proctor-Silex, Nesco, Russell Hobbs, and Breville. These new models include oval slow cookers, sleek chrome versions, and cookers with pre-programmable features.

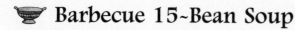 Barbecue 15~Bean Soup

Cooking time: 8 to 10 hours on LOW   4 to 5 hours on HIGH
Attention: Add another ingredient during final hour

This soup really is easy, delicious, and chock full of protein. Serve with crusty bread and garlic butter.

One 20-ounce (560-g) package ham-flavored 15-bean **soup mix**

1 quart (.95 L) water

1 cup (250 g) **barbecue sauce**

2 medium **onions**, chopped

Salt and freshly ground black pepper

Set aside the soup mix seasoning packet and put the beans in a large colander. Pick through the beans to remove any debris, then rinse them under running water. Put the beans in the slow cooker, cover them with water, and let them soak for 6 to 8 hours, or overnight.

Pour the beans back into the colander, discarding the used water, and rinse them under running water. Return the beans to the slow cooker and add 1 quart (.95 L) fresh water. Add the barbecue sauce and chopped onions, and stir to combine. Cover and cook on LOW for 8 to 10 hours or on HIGH for 4 to 5 hours. (Cooking the beans on LOW will bring out the best flavor.)

An hour before the soup is done, add the contents of the soup mix seasoning packet and stir. Just before serving, season the soup with salt and pepper to taste.

YIELD: 8 generous servings

ADD IT! Add 1 pound (455 g) ham, diced, along with the barbecue sauce and chopped onions, and substitute vegetable stock for the water. Reduce the salt accordingly.

NUTRITIONAL ANALYSIS: One serving of the basic recipe contains 103 calories; 2 g fat; 6 g protein; 17 g carbohydrate; and .9 g dietary fiber.

Lentil, Barley, and Sausage Soup

This thick, hearty stew is a protein powerhouse. Serve with mixed vegetables and crusty bread.

> Two 19-ounce (540-g) cans ready-to-eat **lentil soup**
>
> 1 pound (455 g) fresh Italian **sausage**, browned and drained
>
> 1 1/2 cups (355 ml) water
>
> 1 cup (200 g) uncooked **pearl barley**
>
> Salt

Put the lentil soup, browned sausage, water, and barley in the slow cooker and stir to combine. Cover and cook on LOW for 8 to 10 hours.

Before serving, stir the soup and season it with salt to taste.

YIELD: 8 servings

ADD IT! Substitute vegetable broth for the water, and add 2 cloves garlic, minced.

NUTRITIONAL ANALYSIS: One serving of the basic recipe contains 360 calories; 20 g fat; 16 g protein; 31 g carbohydrate; and 4 g dietary fiber.

DON'T TRY THIS

Once you've added all the ingredients, don't stir slow-cooked soups. Lifting the lid throws off the cooking time.

🏺 Wild Rice Soup

Cooking time: 8 to 10 hours on LOW   4 to 5 hours on HIGH
Attention: Minimal

Wild Rice Soup makes an elegant statement. Enjoy this nutty-tasting soup with an open-face cheese sandwich garnished with bacon.

Three 10 3/4-ounce (305-g) cans condensed **cream of mushroom soup**

3 soup cans (918 ml) water

1 1/2 cups (340 g) frozen **Seasoning-Blend Vegetables** (page 30), thawed

1/2 cup (80 g) **wild rice**, boiled for 20 minutes and drained

Salt and freshly ground black pepper

Put the condensed soup, water, Seasoning-Blend Vegetables, and partially cooked wild rice in the slow cooker and stir to combine. Season the mixture with salt and pepper to taste and stir it again. Cook on LOW for 8 to 10 hours or on HIGH for 4 to 5 hours.

YIELD: 8 servings

ADD IT! Substitute 1 quart (.95 L) chicken bouillon for the 3 soup cans water, and add 1 pound (455 g) bacon, cooked and crumbled.

NUTRITIONAL ANALYSIS: One serving of the basic recipe contains 144 calories; 9 g fat; 3 g protein; 14 g carbohydrate; and 2 g dietary fiber.

DID YOU KNOW?

Wild rice isn't really rice—it's a type of aquatic grass that's native to North America.

Wild Rice~Cheese Soup

Cooking time: 2 to 3 1/2 hours
Attention: Stir twice during first 30 minutes; change heat setting and add another ingredient after first 30 minutes

Cheese, potato, and wild-rice flavors merge in this delicious, satisfying soup. Serve with your favorite soup crackers.

7 cups (1.6 L) water

One 9.3-ounce (263-g) package **Fantastic Foods Creamy Potato Simmer Soup**

2 cups (455 g) shredded pasteurized **processed cheese food**

1 cup (160 g) **wild rice**, boiled for 40 minutes and drained

Salt and freshly ground pepper to taste

Put the water and soup mix in the slow cooker and stir until the soup mix has dissolved. Add the cheese food and stir well. Cover and cook on HIGH for 30 minutes, or until the cheese has melted, stirring every 15 minutes.

Add the partially cooked wild rice to the slow cooker and stir again. Reduce the heat to LOW, cover, and cook for 1 1/2 to 3 hours, or until the flavors have melded.

Stir the soup and season it with salt and pepper to taste. Serve the soup warm with crusty bread.

YIELD: 10 servings

ADD IT! Substitute 7 cups (1.6 L) chicken bouillon for the water, and add 1 pound (455 g) bacon, cooked and crumbled.

NUTRITIONAL ANALYSIS: One serving of the basic recipe contains 348 calories; 20 g fat; 21 g protein; 27 g carbohydrate; and 1 g dietary fiber.

🍲 Creamy Potato Soup

Cooking time: 4 to 5 hours on HIGH

Attention: Add another ingredient during final hour

This creamy soup benefits from the essence of the herbs in the soup mix. Ladle into bowls, garnish with fresh chives, and serve with crusty bread.

1 1/2 quarts (1.4 L) water

One 9.3-ounce (263-g) package **Fantastic Foods Creamy Potato Simmer Soup**

4 large **potatoes**, peeled and cut into 1-inch (2.5-cm) cubes

One 12-ounce (355-ml) can **evaporated milk**

Salt and freshly ground black pepper

Put the water and soup mix in the slow cooker and stir until the soup mix has dissolved. Add the potato cubes and stir again. Cover and cook on HIGH for 4 to 5 hours.

An hour before the soup is done, stir in the evaporated milk. Just before serving, season the soup with salt and pepper to taste and stir it again.

YIELD: 8 generous servings

ADD IT! Add 5 1/2 tablespoons (1/2 cup, or 75 g) butter, melted, along with the evaporated milk for a richer-tasting soup.

NUTRITIONAL ANALYSIS: One serving of the basic recipe contains 223 calories; 9 g fat; 11 g protein; 33 g carbohydrate; and 2 g dietary fiber.

 # Potato Minestrone

Cooking time: 8 $1/2$ to 10 $1/2$ hours on LOW   4 $1/2$ to 6 $1/2$ hours on HIGH

Attention: Add another ingredient during final 30 minutes

A satisfying, comfort-food twist on a vegetarian staple. Serve with bruschetta topped with diced tomatoes and chopped fresh basil.

> Three 19-ounce (540-g) cans ready-to-eat **minestrone soup**
>
> 4 large **potatoes**, peeled and cut into 1-inch (2.5-cm) cubes
>
> One 10-ounce (280-g) package **frozen chopped spinach**, thawed and drained

Put the minestrone soup and potato cubes in the slow cooker and stir to combine. Cover and cook on LOW for 8 to 10 hours or on HIGH for 4 to 6 hours.

Add the thawed spinach to the slow cooker and stir again. Cover and cook for another 30 minutes, or until the spinach is hot.

YIELD: 10 generous servings

ADD IT! To pump up the protein content, add a 16-ounce (455-g) can kidney or garbanzo beans, rinsed and drained.

NUTRITIONAL ANALYSIS: One serving of the basic recipe contains 100 calories; 2 g fat; 5 g protein; 17 g carbohydrate; and 2 g dietary fiber.

SAFETY FIRST!

Never immerse a slow cooker in water. If your slow cooker has a stoneware insert, you can remove and wash it as you would any piece of crockery. But clean the appliance itself with a damp rag—and make sure you unplug it first!

Asparagus Soup

Cooking time: 5 1/2 to 7 hours

Attention: Change heat setting, process soup, and add another ingredient during final 30 to 60 minutes

Tender, flavorful baby asparagus in a delicate broth. Add a dollop of sour cream for garnish.

   1 1/2 pounds (683 g) fresh **baby asparagus**, washed and dried

   1 quart (.95 L) **vegetable broth**

   1/4 teaspoon salt

   1/4 teaspoon freshly ground black pepper

Prepare the asparagus by cutting off the tips and setting them aside. Snap off the tough lower ends and discard them. Cut the remaining stems into 1-inch (2.5-cm) pieces and put them in the slow cooker. Add the vegetable broth, salt, and pepper, and stir to combine. Cover and cook on LOW for 5 to 6 hours.

Turn the heat OFF and allow the slow cooker to cool enough so that you can handle the ceramic pot safely. Using a blender or food processor, purée the soup in small batches, returning the puréed soup to the slow cooker. Add the raw asparagus tips and stir to combine. Cover and cook on HIGH for 30 to 60 minutes, or until the asparagus tips are tender.

Serve the soup hot, garnished with a sprinkling of freshly ground black pepper.

YIELD: 6 servings

ADD IT! For a richer soup, add any combination of the following along with the asparagus tips: 1 cup (225 g) diced potatoes, 1/2 cup (75 g) chopped scallions, 1 to 2 cloves garlic, minced. Increase the cooking time by 1 hour.

NUTRITIONAL ANALYSIS: One serving of the basic recipe contains 122 calories; 3 g fat; 5 g protein; 20 g carbohydrate; and 3 g dietary fiber.

☕ Broccoli-Cheese Soup

Cooking time: 4 1/2 to 6 1/2 hours

Attention: Change heat setting and add another ingredient during final 15 to 30 minutes

Smooth and satisfying, this soup is a lovely light meal or a delicious accompaniment. Serve with soft honey wheat rolls.

2 large stalks fresh **broccoli**, washed and dried

Two 10 3/4-ounce (305-g) cans condensed **cream of celery soup**

1 cup (235 ml) water

1 pound (455 g) pasteurized **processed cheese food**, cut into cubes

Salt and freshly ground black pepper

Prepare the broccoli by cutting off the florets and setting them aside. Cut off the tough lower ends and discard them. Cut the remaining stems into rounds or chunks of uniform size and set them aside. The florets and stem pieces should total about 2 1/2 cups (175 g).

Put the condensed soup and water in the slow cooker and stir to combine. Add the broccoli stem pieces and cheese, and stir again. Cover and cook on LOW for 4 to 6 hours, or until the stem pieces are tender but not overcooked.

Turn the heat to HIGH, add the broccoli florets, and stir. Cover and cook for another 15 to 30 minutes, or just until the florets are tender. Season the soup with salt and pepper to taste and serve it immediately.

YIELD: 8 servings

TIP: To save time, steam the broccoli florets before adding them to the soup, and keep the heat on LOW.

ADD IT! For a richer soup, substitute milk for the water.

NUTRITIONAL ANALYSIS: One serving of the basic recipe contains 340 calories; 24 g fat; 20 g protein; 17 g carbohydrate; and 2 g dietary fiber.

🍲 Golden Onion Soup

Cooking time: 5 1/2 to 6 1/2 hours on LOW   2 1/2 to 3 1/2 hours on HIGH
Attention: Minimal

Rich and creamy, this soup is the perfect comfort food for a bone-chilling day. Enjoy with crusty French bread.

- 3 cups (680 g) thinly sliced **onion**
- 4 tablespoons (55 g) **butter**
- Three 2.6-ounce (73-g) envelopes golden **onion soup mix**
- 7 cups (1.6 L) water

In a large skillet over medium heat, sauté the onion in the butter until the onion is translucent; do not allow it to burn.

Put the water and soup mix in the slow cooker and stir until the soup mix has dissolved. Add the sautéed onion and stir again. Cover and cook on LOW for 5 1/2 to 6 1/2 hours or on HIGH for 2 1/2 to 3 1/2 hours.

YIELD: 8 servings

ADD IT! Add 1/4 cup (60 ml) dry vermouth or cognac along with the water.

NUTRITIONAL ANALYSIS: One serving of the basic recipe contains 111 calories; 7 g fat; 2 g protein; 12 g carbohydrate; and 2 g dietary fiber.

TRY THIS

Add a dollop of sour cream or crème fraiche and a sprinkle of chopped chives to each bowl just before serving.

🏺 Cheddar Cheese Soup

Cooking time: 1 1/2 to 2 hours
Attention: Watch to keep from boiling

This rich and creamy soup is fun and fabulous when served in an edible bread bowl. Add heaping servings of steamed California vegetables for a satisfying, balanced meal.

1 pint (475 ml) hot water

2 chicken or vegetable **bouillon cubes**

Two 10 3/4-ounce (305-g) cans condensed **cheddar cheese soup**

3 tablespoons (42 ml) **cooking sherry**

Put the hot water and bouillon cubes in the slow cooker and stir until the bouillon cubes have dissolved. Add the condensed soup and stir again. Cover and cook on LOW for 1 1/2 to 2 hours, or until the soup is hot; do not allow it to boil.

Before serving, add the sherry and stir to combine.

YIELD: 5 servings

NUTRITIONAL ANALYSIS: One serving of the basic recipe contains 137 calories; 7 g fat; 5 g protein; 9 g carbohydrate; and .8 g dietary fiber.

Chapter 9

• •

Sauces, Dressings, and Toppings

Sauces, dressings, and toppings are the accessories of the food world. They add a dash of color, a little excitement, and lots of flavor. Enjoy decorating meat, main dishes, breakfast foods, and desserts with these edible accessories, and you'll have a truly gourmet look for your table.

🥘 Red Pasta Sauce

Cooking time: 2 to 4 hours on LOW	1 to 2 hours on HIGH

Attention: Minimal

This is a delicious way to serve a family favorite. Serve over spaghetti or linguini, with a romaine salad and garlic breadsticks on the side.

One 28-ounce (795-g) jar mushroom-and-garlic-flavored **pasta sauce**

1/3 cup (78 ml) dry **red wine**

1/8 teaspoon crushed **red pepper**

Salt and freshly ground black pepper

Put the pasta sauce and red wine in the slow cooker and stir to combine. Cover and cook on LOW for 2 to 4 hours or on HIGH for 1 to 2 hours.

Before serving, stir the crushed red pepper into the sauce. Season the sauce with salt and black pepper to taste and stir it again.

YIELD: 6 servings

NUTRITIONAL ANALYSIS: One serving of the basic recipe contains 10 calories; trace fat; trace protein; .2 g carbohydrate; and trace dietary fiber.

TRY THIS

Spray a little nonstick cooking spray inside your slow cooker insert before adding ingredients, and gunk wipes off easily after cooking.

🍲 Ginger-Apricot-Cranberry Sauce

A holiday favorite with a kick. Apricots and fresh ginger add an interesting heat to this chilled standard, as cold and refreshing as the winter wind.

One 6-ounce (168-g) package **dried apricots**

One 16-ounce (455-g) can whole-berry **cranberry sauce**

2 tablespoons (28 ml) water

1 tablespoon (6 g) minced fresh **ginger**

Cut the dried apricots into 3 strips each and put them in the slow cooker. Add the cranberry sauce, water, and minced ginger, and stir to combine. Cover and cook on LOW for 3 to 4 hours, or until the apricots are tender and all the flavors have melded.

Allow the sauce to cool to room temperature, then transfer it to an airtight container and refrigerate it until it's very cold. To serve, spoon the sauce into a chilled serving bowl and serve it immediately.

YIELD: 6 servings

NUTRITIONAL ANALYSIS: One serving of the basic recipe contains 182 calories; .2 g fat; 1 g protein; 47 g carbohydrate; and 3 g dietary fiber.

TRY THIS

Reduce the sugar in this dish by substituting from-scratch cranberry sauce for the canned version. Put a 12-ounce (340-g) bag of fresh cranberries, 1/2 cup (60 ml) reduced-sugar cranberry juice, and 1/2 cup plus 1 tablespoon (14 g) Splenda granular no-calorie sweetener in the slow cooker and stir to combine. Cover and cook on HIGH for 3 to 4 hours, or until the cranberries have popped and the syrup has thickened.

Cranberry-Rhubarb Sauce

The slightly sweet and tangy flavor of rhubarb is enhanced by the addition of cranberries. Serve over ice cream or as an accompaniment to fish, scallops, or pork tenderloin.

   1 1/2 pounds (683 g) fresh **rhubarb**, cut into 1/2-inch (1.3-cm) pieces

   12 ounces (340 g) fresh **cranberries**

   1 1/2 cups (300 g) **sugar**

   1/2 cup (120 ml) water

   1/4 teaspoon salt

Put the rhubarb pieces, fresh cranberries, sugar, water, and salt in the slow cooker and stir to combine. Cover and cook on LOW for 4 to 5 hours.

Allow the sauce to cool to room temperature, then transfer it to an airtight container and refrigerate it until it's very cold. Serve it chilled.

YIELD: 6 servings

NUTRITIONAL ANALYSIS: One serving of the basic recipe contains 239 calories; 0 g fat; 1 g protein; 61 g carbohydrate; and 4 g dietary fiber.

TRY THIS

To create a rich, exotic flavor, stir in a tablespoon or two (to taste) of peach or apricot chutney in the last half-hour of cooking.

Easy Barbecue Sauce

Cooking time: 1 to 2 hours	Attention: Minimal

When you're caught short and don't have time to run to the store, this quick and easy recipe for barbecue sauce will do the trick.

  3 cups (720 g) **ketchup**

  1/4 cup (63 g) **honey mustard sauce**

  1/4 cup (60 ml) **apple cider vinegar**

  1/8 teaspoon freshly ground black pepper

Put the ketchup, honey mustard sauce, apple cider vinegar, and pepper in the slow cooker and stir to combine. Cover and cook on LOW for 1 to 2 hours, or until the flavors have melded.

YIELD: 6 servings

ADD IT! Add 1 clove garlic, minced. To sweeten the sauce, add honey to taste.

NUTRITIONAL ANALYSIS: One serving of the basic recipe contains 150 calories; 3 g fat; 2 g protein; 35 g carbohydrate; and 2 g dietary fiber.

Favorite Barbecue Sauce

Cooking time: 1 to 2 hours	Attention: Minimal

Ready for a change? Take your favorite barbecue sauce and reinvent it!

  2 cups (500 g) bottled **barbecue sauce**

  1/2 cup (170 g) **honey**

Put the bottled barbecue sauce and honey in the slow cooker and stir to combine. Cover and cook on LOW for 1 to 2 hours, or until the flavors have melded.

YIELD: 5 servings

NUTRITIONAL ANALYSIS: One serving of the basic recipe contains 178 calories; 2 g fat; 2 g protein; 41 g carbohydrate; and 1 g dietary fiber.

 **Dressed~Up Barbecue Sauce**

Cooking time: 1 to 2 hours	**Attention:** Minimal

Sometimes on holiday weekends, all that the supermarket shelves yield is store-brand barbecue sauce. Try this little pick-me-up, and your family will think you picked up gourmet barbecue sauce instead.

   2 cups (500 g) **barbecue sauce**

   $^1/_4$ cup (56 g) dark **brown sugar**, packed

   4 tablespoons (55 g) **butter**, melted

   $^1/_8$ teaspoon freshly ground black pepper

Put the bottled barbecue sauce, brown sugar, melted butter, and pepper in the slow cooker and stir to combine. Cover and cook on LOW for 1 to 2 hours, or until the flavors have melded.

YIELD: 5 servings

ADD IT! Add 1 clove garlic, minced, and 1 tablespoon (15 g) hot sauce for an extra kick.

NUTRITIONAL ANALYSIS: One serving of the basic recipe contains 198 calories; 11 g fat; 2 g protein; 24 g carbohydrate; and 1 g dietary fiber.

TRY THIS

This sauce also makes a phenomenal layer in a ground beef (or chicken) dip. Pour it over cooked and drained ground beef or chicken in a casserole dish, top with grated Monterey jack or Swiss cheese, and all you need is tortilla chips for dipping—and maybe some beer or margaritas!

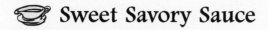 # Sweet Savory Sauce

Cooking time: 1¹/₂ to 2¹/₂ hours	**Attention:** Minimal

A special sauce that's easy to make and tastes great with just about anything. Try drowning cooked cocktail franks, hot dogs, pork morsels, meatballs, or chicken wings in a slow cooker full of this sauce. A real crowd pleaser.

> 1 cup (225 g) **chili sauce**
> 1 cup currant (320 g) **jelly**
> 1 tablespoon (15 g) **Dijon mustard**

Put the chili sauce, currant jelly, and mustard in the slow cooker and stir to combine. Cover and cook on LOW for 1¹/₂ to 2¹/₂ hours, or until the flavors have melded.

Serve the sauce warm from the slow cooker.

YIELD: 5 servings

ADD IT! For a richer sauce, add 1 ounce (28 ml) dry red wine.

NUTRITIONAL ANALYSIS: One serving of the basic recipe contains 177 calories; 0 g fat; 1 g protein; 46 g carbohydrate; and 2 g dietary fiber.

SPEED IT UP

If this sauce will be served with appetizer meats, heat the meat in the sauce and serve it from the slow cooker. This sauce is enough for 1 to 1¹/₂ pounds (455 to 683 g) of meat.

🍲 Mustard Sauce

Cooking time: 1 to 2 hours   **Attention:** Minimal

A quick-and-easy solution to humdrum pork chops and ribs.

    1 cup (225 g) **brown sugar**, packed

    1 cup (240 g) **honey mustard**

    1 cup (235 ml) **apple cider vinegar** or **beer**

Put the brown sugar, honey mustard, and apple cider vinegar in the slow cooker and stir to combine. Cover and cook on LOW for 1 to 2 hours, or until all the flavors have melded. Use this sauce as a pork or rib finishing sauce, as a table sauce, or on sandwiches.

YIELD: 6 servings

NUTRITIONAL ANALYSIS: One serving of the basic recipe (made with apple cider vinegar) contains 174 calories; 2 g fat; 2 g protein; 41 g carbohydrate; and 1 g dietary fiber.

🍲 Herb Stuffing

Cooking time: 4 to 5 hours   **Attention:** Minimal

It's a cinch to prepare stuffing outside the turkey using your slow cooker.

    1 1/2 cups (340 g) frozen **Seasoning-Blend Vegetables** (page 30)

    4 tablespoons (55 g) **butter**

    One 14-ounce (398-g) package bread cube style **herb-seasoned stuffing mix**

    1 1/2 pints (710 ml) water

Spray the inside of the slow cooker with cooking spray.

In a large skillet over medium heat, sauté the Seasoning-Blend Vegetables in the butter until the onion is translucent. Place the sautéed vegetables in the slow cooker along with the stuffing mix and stir to combine. Sprinkle the water over the vegetable-and-stuffing mixture and mix lightly. Cover and cook on LOW for 4 to 5 hours.

YIELD: 8 servings

ADD IT! Substitute 1 1/2 cups (355 ml) applesauce or chicken bouillon for an equal amount of the water. Garnish the stuffing with toasted chopped walnuts.

NUTRITIONAL ANALYSIS: One serving of the basic recipe contains 259 calories; 8 g fat; 6 g protein; 41 g carbohydrate; and 3 g dietary fiber.

🍲 Curried Fruit Topping

Cooking time: 6 to 8 hours on LOW   3 to 4 hours on HIGH
Attention: Minimal

You can prepare hot curried fruit using a variety of fruits. Some of the most popular are peaches, pineapples, pears, cherries, and apricots. Enjoy with yogurt for breakfast or with ice cream any time.

    4 cups (856 g) assorted **canned fruits**, drained

    ³/4 cup (169 g) **brown sugar**, firmly packed

    1 tablespoon (6 g) **curry powder**

    ¹/4 teaspoon salt

Layer the different canned fruits, one type of fruit per layer, on the bottom of the slow cooker. Combine the brown sugar, curry powder, and salt in a small bowl and sprinkle the mixture over the fruits. Cover and cook on LOW for 6 to 8 hours or on HIGH for 3 to 4 hours.

YIELD: 8 servings

ADD IT! Toast ¹/2 cup (63 g) slivered almonds in 8 tablespoons (1 stick, or 112 g) butter and layer them on the bottom of the slow cooker along with the fruits.

NUTRITIONAL ANALYSIS: One serving of the basic recipe contains 172 calories; 0 g fat; .6 g protein; 45 g carbohydrate; and 2 g dietary fiber.

🥣 Apricot Preserves

Cooking time: 2 1/2 to 5 hours

Attention: Stir every 45 to 60 minutes; remove cover during final 1 to 2 hours

Whether it's summer or winter, the taste of Apricot Preserves is always a welcome treat. Slather it on hot, buttered toast, drizzle it over ice cream, or use it in recipes.

1 pound (455 g) **dried apricots**, finely chopped in a food processor

3 1/2 cups (885 ml) **unsweetened apple juice**

1 cup (200 g) **sugar**

Sterilize a glass jar with a tight-fitting lid and set it aside.

Put the apricot pieces, apple juice, and sugar in the slow cooker and stir to combine. Cover and cook on HIGH for 1 1/2 to 3 hours, stirring every 45 to 60 minutes. Uncover and cook for an additional 1 to 2 hours, or until the mixture has thickened, stirring occasionally.

Ladle the preserves into the prepared jar and allow them to cool. Screw on the lid and store the preserves in the refrigerator.

YIELD: 8 servings

NUTRITIONAL ANALYSIS: One serving of the basic recipe contains 283 calories; 0 g fat; 2 g protein; 73 g carbohydrate; and 5 g dietary fiber.

TRY THIS

Next time you need a quick and delicious frosting on a layer cake, spread this preserves over the bottom layer, add a layer of whipped cream, then the top cake layer, another layer of preserves, and another layer of whipped cream. Serve immediately. Yum!

Chapter 10

• •

Main Dishes:
Beef, Pork, and Other Meats

Bring out the tender, juicy flavor of meat—and do it the easy way. The slow cooker reigns supreme when it comes to preparing meats and meaty stews. Inexpensive tougher cuts almost magically become fall-apart tender. And how delightful that delicious gravies and sauces develop on their own while the meat cooks. The slow cooker captures the abundance of juices and tasty bits of meat as the roast or stew is slowly cooked to perfection. For tricks to make a superior gravy or sauce to accompany your meal, check out the "Tips" or the "Try This" boxes with the recipes.

Beef Burgundy in Hunter Sauce

Cooking time: 8 to 10 hours	**Attention:** Minimal

Simple yet elegant roast beef coddled in a sensational mushroom-onion-wine sauce. Enjoy with garlic potatoes and dinner rolls.

> One 3- to 4-pound (1.4- to 1.8-kg) **beef roast**
>
> $^3/_4$ cup (175 ml) water
>
> $^1/_2$ cup (120 ml) dry **red wine**
>
> One 1.1-ounce (31-g) envelope **hunter sauce mix**

Put the beef roast in the slow cooker. Combine the water, red wine, and sauce mix in a small bowl and pour the mixture over the roast. Cover and cook on LOW for 8 to 10 hours, or until the roast is done.

YIELD: 12 servings

TIP: If you don't have hunter sauce mix on hand, substitute onion-mushroom soup mix.

ADD IT! For an instant side dish, stir 8 ounces (225 g) thickly sliced fresh mushrooms into the sauce mixture. Garnish the finished roast with chopped fresh parsley.

NUTRITIONAL ANALYSIS: One serving of the basic recipe (made with a 3-pound beef roast) contains 251 calories; 18 g fat; 18 g protein; 2 g carbohydrate; and 0 g dietary fiber.

DID YOU KNOW?

Hunter sauce, also called chasseur sauce, is a brown sauce made with tomato purée and flavored with mushrooms, onion, and a hint of white wine. This robust sauce was created in the early 1600s to tenderize tough old game birds. You'll enjoy hunter sauce for its rich, full-bodied taste, but you really won't need it to tenderize your slow-cooked roast.

Spicy Pot Roast with Onions

Cooking time: 8 to 10 hours   **Attention:** Minimal

The rich sauce adds spice and excitement, and puts the finishing touch on this tender roast. Serve the roast with a green salad and crusty bread.

> 2 **onions**, quartered
>
> One 2-pound (910-g) **beef roast**
>
> One 2.25-ounce (63-g) envelope French's onion-flavored **Chili-O Seasoning Mix**
>
> 1/2 cup (120 ml) water

Put the onion quarters in the slow cooker and place the pot roast on top of them. In a small bowl, dissolve the seasoning mix in the water, then pour the mixture over the pot roast. Cover and cook on LOW for 8 to 10 hours, or until the roast is done.

To serve, remove the roast from the slow cooker and place it on a platter. Let it rest for 10 minutes, then carve it into 1/2-inch (6-mm) slices.

YIELD: 8 servings

ADD IT! Add 4 medium tomatoes, peeled and chopped into 1-inch (2.5-cm) pieces, and 1/2 cup (61 g) baby carrots. Arrange the vegetables around the sides of the slow cooker to help them cook faster.

NUTRITIONAL ANALYSIS: One serving of the basic recipe contains 287 calories; 18 g fat; 18 g protein; 10 g carbohydrate; and .8 g dietary fiber.

TRY THIS

To make a great gravy, dissolve 3 tablespoons (24 g) flour in 1/2 cup (120 ml) water and add the mixture to the juices left in the slow cooker after removing the pot roast. Season the gravy with salt and freshly ground black pepper to taste.

 Slow~Cooker Brisket

Cooking time: 8 to 10 hours	**Attention:** Minimal

Brisket is a very tasty cut of meat that's making a big comeback in trendy restaurants. Cooked slowly with moist heat, it's succulent and full-flavored.

- One 3- to 4-pound (1.4- to 1.8-kg) **beef brisket**, or a size that fits inside your covered slow cooker
- Salt and freshly ground black pepper
- One 2-ounce (55-g) envelope **onion soup mix**
- One .9-ounce (25-g) envelope **brown gravy mix**
- 1 ¹/₂ cups (355 ml) water

Put the brisket in the slow cooker fat side up. Season the beef brisket with salt and pepper. In a small bowl, dissolve the soup mix and gravy mix in the water, then pour the mixture over the brisket. Cover and cook on LOW for 8 to 10 hours, or until the brisket is done.

To serve, remove the roast from the slow cooker and place it fat side up on a platter. Let it rest for 10 to 15 minutes, then carve it diagonally across the grain into thin slices.

YIELD: 10 servings

ADD IT! Peel enough potatoes, carrots, and onions to feed your dinner crowd, cut them into uniform-size chunks, and arrange them around the sides of the slow cooker.

NUTRITIONAL ANALYSIS: One serving of the basic recipe (made with a 3-pound beef brisket) contains 451 calories; 37 g fat; 24 g protein; 5 g carbohydrate; and .6 g dietary fiber.

Steak Roll~Ups with Asparagus

Cooking time: 5 to 7 hours	**Attention:** Minimal

The essence of elegance, yet so simple to prepare and cook. Serve with Caesar salad, French bread, and herbed butter.

- 6 cube **steaks**
- ¹/₄ teaspoon salt
- ¹/₂ teaspoon freshly ground black pepper
- 18 baby **asparagus spears**, trimmed
- 12 very small **new potatoes**, scrubbed

Season the cube steaks with the salt and pepper. Position three spears of asparagus on top of each cube steak, then roll up the steaks jelly-roll style. Secure the ends of the rolled-up cube steaks with toothpicks.

Put the potatoes in the slow cooker and place the rolled-up cube steaks seam sides down on top of them. Cover and cook on LOW for 5 to 7 hours.

YIELD: 6 servings

ADD IT! Substitute adobo seasoning for the salt and pepper.

NUTRITIONAL ANALYSIS: One serving of the basic recipe contains 410 calories; 14 g fat; 26 g protein; 46 g carbohydrate; and 5 g dietary fiber.

Three-Alarm Chili

Cooking time: 6 to 8 hours	Attention: Minimal

When it turns cold and wet outside, there's nothing better to warm the bones than Three-Alarm Chili. Serve with your choice of shredded cheese and plenty of beverages to quench the fire.

2 pounds (910 g) **beef chuck**, cut into 1-inch (2.5-cm) cubes

1/2 teaspoon salt

1/4 teaspoon freshly ground black pepper

One 2.25-ounce (63-g) envelope French's Texas-style **Chili-O Seasoning Mix**

One 14 1/2-ounce (413-g) can Mexican-flavored **stewed tomatoes** with jalapeños, garlic, and cumin

Put the beef cubes in the slow cooker and season them on all sides with the salt and pepper. Sprinkle the beef cubes with the seasoning mix, then top them with the stewed tomatoes. Cover and cook on LOW for 6 to 8 hours.

Before serving, stir the chili and season it with additional salt and freshly ground black pepper.

YIELD: 8 servings

ADD IT! Add 5 to 10 drops Tabasco sauce along with the seasoning mix and stewed tomatoes—if you dare!

NUTRITIONAL ANALYSIS: One serving of the basic recipe contains 291 calories; 18 g fat; 19 g protein; 12 g carbohydrate; and .8 g dietary fiber.

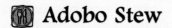 Adobo Stew

What a big payoff for such a small amount of effort! Enjoy this peppery, tender stew with rice and mixed vegetables.

> 1 ¹/₂-pound (683-g) beef or **pork roast**, cut into 1-inch (2.5-cm) cubes
>
> ¹/₂ cup (120 ml) water
>
> ¹/₂ cup (120 ml) **apple cider vinegar**
>
> ¹/₄ cup (60 ml) **soy sauce**
>
> ¹/₄ teaspoon freshly ground black pepper

Put the beef or pork cubes in the slow cooker. In a small bowl, combine the water, apple cider vinegar, soy sauce, and pepper, then pour the mixture over the meat. Cover and cook on LOW for 6 to 8 hours.

Before serving, stir the stew and season it with additional freshly ground black pepper. Serve the stew with rice, either with or without the sauce.

YIELD: 5 servings

ADD IT! If you like the taste of garlic, substitute garlic-flavored soy sauce for the plain soy sauce. If you don't have this gourmet soy sauce on hand, add 2 cloves garlic, minced, to the stew along with the plain soy sauce. For an authentic touch, substitute coconut milk for the water. Throw in a bay leaf for good measure, as long as you remember to remove it before serving the stew.

NUTRITIONAL ANALYSIS: One serving of the basic recipe (made with beef roast) contains 295 calories; 21 g fat; 22 g protein; 3 g carbohydrate; and 0 g dietary fiber.

DID YOU KNOW?

Adobo is the national dish of the Philippines. It'a stew of pork, beef, or chicken cooked in soy sauce and vinegar, with garlic and lots of black pepper. Our version calls for less black pepper, but if you get a hankering to be really authentic, feel free to keep that pepper mill grinding.

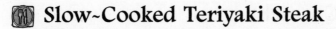 Slow~Cooked Teriyaki Steak

Cooking time: 8 to 10 hours   **Attention:** Minimal

Peanut oil paired with teriyaki sauce adds just the right accent. Serve with rice and sauce from the slow cooker.

    1 pound (455 g) **beef stir-fry strips**
    1 to 2 tablespoons (14 to 28 ml) **peanut oil**
    1 cup (235 ml) **teriyaki sauce**
    1/4 cup (60 ml) water

In a large skillet over medium heat, brown the beef strips in the peanut oil. Drain the browned meat and place it in the slow cooker.

In a small bowl, combine the teriyaki sauce and water, then pour the mixture over the beef strips. Cover and cook on LOW for 8 to 10 hours.

YIELD: 4 servings

ADD IT! Brown the beef strips with any or all of the following: 1/2 cup (33 g) chopped onion, 1 teaspoon minced fresh ginger, 1 clove garlic, minced. Place the cooked seasonings in the slow cooker along with the meat.

NUTRITIONAL ANALYSIS: One serving of the basic recipe (made with 1 tablespoon peanut oil) contains 375 calories; 25 g fat; 25 g protein; 12 g carbohydrate; and trace dietary fiber.

DID YOU KNOW?

The mild flavor of peanut oil really makes a difference when you're cooking an Asian-inspired dish. A good cold-pressed peanut oil will have the aroma of freshly roasted peanuts. Preserve the flavor and aroma by storing the oil in the refrigerator or in another cold, dark location.

Lazy~Day Cheeseburgers

Lazy days can produce the most delicious meals. Enjoy this cheesy burger mixture on onion buns.

1 1/4 pounds (569 g) **ground beef**

1/4 teaspoon salt

1/8 teaspoon freshly ground black pepper

8 ounces (225 g) pasteurized **processed cheese food**, grated

8 onion-flavored **sandwich buns**

In a large skillet over medium heat, brown the ground beef. Drain the browned meat and season with the salt and pepper. Put the browned meat in the slow cooker, add the cheese, and stir to combine. Cover and cook on LOW for 6 to 7 hours.

Spoon the burger mixture onto the buns, and serve the sandwiches with plenty of dinner napkins.

YIELD: 8 servings

ADD IT! Brown the ground beef with 1/2 cup (43 g) chopped onion and 1 clove garlic, minced.

NUTRITIONAL ANALYSIS: One serving of the basic recipe contains 454 calories; 31g fat; 23 g protein; 22 g carbohydrate; and .9 g dietary fiber.

TRY THIS

Add a blast of flavor by putting a dollop of gourmet ketchup or mustard, chutney, or green chile sauce (or some sliced jalapenos) on top of the burger mixture. A red cabbage or broccoli slaw makes a crunchy, colorful accompaniment.

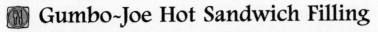 Gumbo~Joe Hot Sandwich Filling

Cooking time: 4 to 6 hours on LOW   2 to 3 hours on HIGH
Attention: Minimal

Not your ordinary sloppy sandwich. Try, instead, a little something Cajun for your sandwich bun.

One 10³/4-ounce (305-g) can condensed **chicken gumbo soup**

¹/2 cup (120 g) **ketchup**

2 pounds (910 g) **ground beef**, browned and drained

Salt and freshly ground black pepper

Put the condensed soup and ketchup in the slow cooker and stir to combine. Add the browned meat and stir again. Cover and cook on LOW for 4 to 6 hours or on HIGH for 2 to 3 hours.

Stir the mixture and season it with salt and pepper to taste. Serve it on toasted sandwich buns, with a side of coleslaw.

YIELD: 10 servings

ADD IT! Add ¹/2 cup (113 g) frozen Seasoning-Blend Vegetables (page 30), 2 tablespoons (30 g) prepared yellow mustard, and ¹/2 teaspoon Cajun seasoning to the soup-and-ketchup mixture.

NUTRITIONAL ANALYSIS: One serving of the basic recipe contains 314 calories; 25 g fat; 17 g protein; 6 g carbohydrate; and .3 g dietary fiber.

DID YOU KNOW?

No one is sure whether the word "gumbo" derives from an African word for okra, "gombo," or a Choctaw word for the spice file (made from dried sassafras leaves), "kombo." Both are ingredients in what we know as gumbo.

Fiesta Meatballs

Jalapeños and cumin lend a distinctive southwestern flare to this party favorite. Serve over Spanish rice or Yellow Rice (page 225), with a side of tortilla chips. Leftover meatballs on buns make awesome next-day sandwiches.

One 14 1/2-ounce (413-g) can Mexican-flavored **stewed tomatoes** with jalapeños, garlic, and cumin

1 small green **bell pepper**, chopped

1/4 teaspoon salt

1 1/4 pounds (569 g) frozen fully cooked **meatballs**, completely thawed

Put the stewed tomatoes, chopped green pepper, and salt in the slow cooker and stir to combine. Add the thawed meatballs and stir again. Cover and cook on LOW for 3 1/2 to 4 1/2 hours or on HIGH for 1 to 2 hours, or until the sauce is hot and thickened.

YIELD: 5 servings

NUTRITIONAL ANALYSIS: One serving of the basic recipe contains 378 calories; 30 g fat; 16 g protein; 15 g carbohydrate; and 4 g dietary fiber.

TRY THIS

Pass the crudités! To add some crunch (not to mention vitamins) to your fiesta, make a platter of red, yellow, and orange pepper rings, cherry tomatoes, broccoli bites, and sliced cucumbers. Let family and friends help themselves. End the meal with refreshing sliced melon.

Slow~Cooker Sausage and Lima Beans

The mild flavor of limas and the spicy flavor of sausage are perfect counter-parts. Serve with biscuits and honey butter.

- 2 cups (475 ml) hot water
- 2 beef **bouillon cubes**
- 1 to 1 1/2 pounds (455 to 683 g) **smoked sausage**, sliced into 1/2-inch (1.3-cm) coins
- One 15-ounce (417-g) can baby **lima beans**, drained
- 1/2 teaspoon freshly ground black pepper

Put the hot water and bouillon cubes in the slow cooker and stir until the bouillon cubes have dissolved. Add the sausage coins and lima beans, and stir again. Cover and cook on LOW for 8 to 10 hours.

Before serving, stir the mixture and season it with the pepper.

YIELD: 8 servings

ADD IT! Add 1/2 cup (60 g) chopped green onion, 1 clove garlic, minced, and hot sauce to taste along with the sausage coins and lima beans.

NUTRITIONAL ANALYSIS: One serving of the basic recipe (made with 1 pound smoked sausage) contains 371 calories; 18 g fat; 19 g protein; 35 g carbohydrate; and 11 g dietary fiber.

DID YOU KNOW?

Lima beans, also called butter beans, are a favorite southern staple. Fordhooks are the large variety and slightly stronger in taste. Baby limas are a smaller, milder variety, not just small Fordhooks. Choose your beans accordingly!

Pork Roast with 40 Cloves of Garlic

Succulent pork roast with mellow, sweet garlic tastes great sliced thin and served with gravy. Enjoy with a baked-apple dessert.

40 cloves **garlic**, peeled

One 2- to 3-pound (.9- to 1.4-kg) boneless **pork loin roast, boneless**

One 10³/4-ounce (305-g) can condensed **cream of mushroom soup**

Put the garlic cloves in the slow cooker, spreading them out to form a single layer. Place the pork roast on top of the garlic cloves and pour the condensed soup over the pork. Cover and cook for 6 to 8 hours on LOW, or until the roast is done.

YIELD: 8 servings

NUTRITIONAL ANALYSIS: One serving of the basic recipe (made with a 2-pound pork roast) contains 230 calories; 14 g fat; 19 g protein; 8 g carbohydrate; and .4 g dietary fiber.

TRY THIS

You can purchase jars of whole garlic cloves in oil, or you can peel your own. If you've never peeled garlic before, try this method: Press the head of garlic on your countertop until the cloves begin to separate. Remove 40 cloves and toss them into a pot of boiling water for just a few seconds. Allow them to cool, then slip off their peels. Slice the root end off each clove, and you're done!

To make a great gravy, dissolve 3 tablespoons (24 g) flour in ¹/2 cup (120 ml) water and add the mixture to the juices left in the slow cooker after the pork roast has been removed. Season the gravy with salt and freshly ground black pepper to taste.

 Pulled~Pork Barbecue

Cooking time: 8 to 10 hours   **Attention:** Minimal

Fall-apart goodness that you shred with a fork. Serve on a sandwich bun, accompanied by coleslaw and potato salad.

> One 3-pound (1.4-kg) **pork loin roast, boneless**, or a size that fits inside your covered slow cooker
>
> 1 1/2 cups (375 g) **barbecue sauce**

In a large skillet over medium heat, sear the pork roast on all sides. Place the pork roast in the slow cooker and drizzle it with the barbecue sauce. Cover and cook on LOW for 8 to 10 hours.

Shred the pork roast with a fork and serve it on sandwich buns.

YIELD: 8 servings

NUTRITIONAL ANALYSIS: One serving of the basic recipe contains 287 calories; 17 g fat; 26 g protein; 6 g carbohydrate; and .7 g dietary fiber.

DID YOU KNOW?

Pulled pork, pork smoked until the meat was tender enough to pull apart by hand, was the first barbecue. Nowadays it's also considered okay to pull it into shreds with a fork!

 Creamy Pork Tenderloin

Cooking time: 8 to 10 hours   **Attention:** Minimal

Garlic-flavored mushrooms and pork make for a tasty and tender main dish.
Serve with baked potatoes and a green salad.

  1 1/4 pounds (569 g) **pork tenderloin**

  1 teaspoon **adobo seasoning**, with salt and with or without black pepper

  Two 10 3/4-ounce (305-g) cans **condensed cream of mushroom soup**

  Salt and freshly ground black pepper

Season the pork tenderloin on all sides with the adobo seasoning, then place the tenderloin in the slow cooker. Pour the condensed soup over the tenderloin, covering it completely. Cover and cook on LOW for 8 to 10 hours.

Place the tenderloin on a platter and season it with salt and pepper to taste. Serve it with the extra gravy on the side.

YIELD: 5 servings

ADD IT! For a more garlicky sauce, substitute condensed cream of mushroom with roasted garlic soup for the plain soup.

NUTRITIONAL ANALYSIS: One serving of the basic recipe contains 264 calories; 13 g fat; 26 g protein; 9 g carbohydrate; and .4 g dietary fiber.

DID YOU KNOW?

Adobo seasoning is definitely in the running for best-kept-secret ingredient. A traditional and popular spice mix from Mexico, it's well balanced, spicy, and rich in flavor, but not hot. Adobo seasoning comes in various combinations—with or without salt and/or black pepper—so read the label before you buy. What you can count on it containing is garlic, onion, Mexican oregano, cumin, and cayenne red pepper.

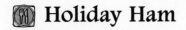 Holiday Ham

Cooking time: 6 to 8 hours   **Attention:** Minimal

This quick-and-easy ham will get raves. Don't let on how little time it really took to prepare.

> 2 1/2- to 4-pound (1.1- to 1.8-kg) **ham**, or a size that fits inside your covered slow cooker
>
> 2 cups (498 g) canned **pineapple chunks**, undrained
>
> 1/2 cup (161 g) pure **maple syrup**

Put the ham in the slow cooker. Pour the pineapple chunks over the ham and then drizzle on the maple syrup. Cover and cook on LOW for 6 to 8 hours.

Serve the ham with the pineapple chunks on the side.

YIELD: 10 servings

NUTRITIONAL ANALYSIS: One serving of the basic recipe (made with a 2 1/2-pound ham) contains 278 calories; 12 g fat; 20 g protein; 22 g carbohydrate; and .4 g dietary fiber.

TRY THIS

For a fancier presentation, you can attach pineapple rings and candied cherries to the ham with cloves before serving.

Coddled Ham

Cooking time: 6 to 10 hours on LOW   3 to 5 hours on HIGH
Attention: Minimal

Indulge yourself with this easy-to-prepare ham. With very little effort, you can prepare a wonderful meal and win yourself a day away from the kitchen.

> 1/2 cup (120 ml) water
>
> 1/2 cup (120 ml) **ham glaze**
>
> One 3- to 4-pound (1.4- to 1.8-kg) fully cooked **ham**, or a size that fits inside your covered slow cooker

Pour the water into the slow cooker. Rub the ham glaze over the ham, wrap and seal the ham in aluminum foil, and place it in the water. Cover and cook on LOW for 6 to 10 hours or on HIGH for 3 to 5 hours, or until the ham is hot throughout; do not overcook the ham or it may fall apart when sliced.

YIELD: 12 servings

NUTRITIONAL ANALYSIS: One serving of the basic recipe (made with a 3-pound ham) contains 227 calories; 12 g fat; 20 g protein; 9 g carbohydrate; and 0 g dietary fiber.

Easiest Ribs

Cooking time: 8 to 9 hours   **Attention:** Minimal

The unusual blend of flavors in this recipe creates a tasty and memorable main dish. Serve with buttered corn-on-the-cob and coleslaw.

> 1 slab **pork ribs** in a size that fits inside your covered slow cooker
>
> One 12-ounce (340-g) bottle **chili sauce**
>
> One 10-ounce (280-g) jar **currant jelly**

Put the ribs in the slow cooker. In a medium-size bowl, combine the chili sauce and currant jelly, then pour the mixture over the ribs. Cover and cook on LOW for 8 to 9 hours.

YIELD: 8 servings

NUTRITIONAL ANALYSIS: One serving of the basic recipe (made with 4 pounds pork ribs) contains 531 calories; 28 g fat; 41 g protein; 27 g carbohydrate; and 1g dietary fiber.

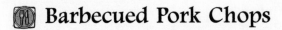 Barbecued Pork Chops

Cooking time: 8 to 10 hours   **Attention:** Minimal

Succulent and saucy, these pork chops will melt in your mouth. Enjoy with green vegetables and 7-grain bread.

Four 1/2-inch (1.9-cm)–thick **pork loin** chops

One 8-ounce (225-g) can **tomato sauce**

1/2 cup (125 g) hickory smoke–flavored **barbecue sauce**

1/2 teaspoon freshly ground black pepper

Put the pork chops in the slow cooker. In a medium-size bowl, combine the tomato sauce, barbecue sauce, and pepper, then pour the mixture over the pork chops. Cover and cook on LOW for 8 to 10 hours.

YIELD: 4 servings

ADD IT! Add 1/2 cup (28 g) minced onion, 1 teaspoon dried oregano, and 2 cloves garlic, minced, to the sauce mixture.

NUTRITIONAL ANALYSIS: One serving of the basic recipe contains 169 calories; 6 g fat; 20 g protein; 8 g carbohydrate; and 1 g dietary fiber.

TRY THIS

This recipe also makes delicious barbecued chicken wings. Add 8 to 12 wings instead of the chops and enjoy!

Pork Chops and Vegetables in Mushroom Gravy

Cooking time: 7 1/2 to 8 1/2 hours on LOW   3 1/2 to 4 1/2 hours on HIGH
Attention: Minimal

A truly smooth and savory one-pot meal. Mushrooms pair well with the vegetables and the pork.

6 cups (720 g) frozen **stew vegetables**, thawed

6 pork **loin chops**, trimmed

Salt and freshly ground black pepper

One 10 3/4-ounce (305-g) can condensed **cream of mushroom soup**

1/4 cup (60 ml) water

Put the vegetables in the slow cooker. Lightly season the pork chops with salt and pepper on both sides and place them on top of the vegetables. In a small bowl, combine the condensed soup and water, then pour the mixture over the pork chops. Cover and cook on LOW for 7 1/2 to 8 1/2 hours or on HIGH for 3 1/2 to 4 1/2 hours.

YIELD: 6 servings

ADD IT! Substitute white wine or chicken broth for the water.

NUTRITIONAL ANALYSIS: One serving of the basic recipe contains 212 calories; 7 g fat; 13 g protein; 28 g carbohydrate; and 8 g dietary fiber.

TRY THIS

Enjoy these rich, satisfying chops with a crusty loaf of bread, a spinach salad, and your favorite wine.

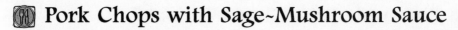 # Pork Chops with Sage~Mushroom Sauce

Cooking time: 8 to 10 hours	**Attention:** Minimal

Sage and mushrooms combine to give pork chops a new flavor your guests won't soon forget. Serve with wild rice and sourdough bread.

8 thick boneless **pork chops**

1 1/4 (8 g) teaspoons salt

1/4 teaspoon freshly ground black pepper

1/4 teaspoon ground **sage**

Onew 10 3/4-ounce (305-g) can condensed **cream of mushroom soup**

In a large nonstick skillet, sear each pork chop on both sides, adding a small amount of water to the pan, if necessary; do not discard the pan juices. Drain the seared chops, season them on both sides with the salt and pepper, and place them in the slow cooker. Sprinkle the chops with the sage.

Pour the condensed soup into the skillet, stir to combine it with the pan juices, and pour the mixture over the pork chops. Cover and cook on LOW for 8 to 10 hours.

YIELD: 8 servings

NUTRITIONAL ANALYSIS: One serving of the basic recipe contains 264 calories; 17 g fat; 24 g protein; 2 g carbohydrate; and .1 g dietary fiber.

TRY THIS

It's easy to grow your own fresh sage. Buy a plant with plain gray-green leaves (they taste better than the multicolored varieties), and plant it in a well-drained, sunny spot. Harvest individual leaves as needed.

Pineapple Pork Chops Teriyaki

Cooking time: 6 to 8 hours   **Attention:** Minimal

Sweet-and-sour pork chops are a luscious, tender treat. Serve over rice and top with the pineapple sauce.

  6 **pork chops**, browned, if desired

  One 15-ounce (417-g) can **pineapple tidbits**, undrained

  3 tablespoons (45 ml) **teriyaki sauce**

Put the pork chops in the slow cooker. In a medium-size bowl, combine the pineapple tidbits and teriyaki sauce, then pour the mixture over the pork chops. Cover and cook on LOW for 6 to 8 hours.

Serve the pork chops with the pineapple sauce.

YIELD: 6 servings

ADD IT! Add 1/2 teaspoon minced fresh ginger and 1 clove garlic, minced, to the pineapple-teriyaki mixture. Serve the pork chops garnished with chopped green onion.

NUTRITIONAL ANALYSIS: One serving of the basic recipe contains 282 calories; 15 g fat; 24 g protein; 13 g carbohydrate; and .5 g dietary fiber.

IT'S GOOD FOR YOU

The enzyme bromelain in pineapple fights inflammation, so it helps relieve a host of problems from bruises and swelling to rheumatoid arthritis. It also promotes faster healing. And pineapple is also a great source of vitamin C.

 # Creamy Pork Chops

Cooking time: 8 to 10 hours	**Attention:** Minimal

This recipe makes a rich mushroom sauce that pairs well with both mashed potatoes and rice. Add a green vegetable and yeasty dinner rolls for a complete meal.

> One 10 3/4-ounce (305-g) can **condensed golden mushroom soup**
>
> 1/3 cup (78 ml) good **white wine** or **cooking wine**
>
> 4 **pork chops**

Put the condensed soup and wine in the slow cooker and stir to combine. Add the pork chops and turn them to coat them with the sauce. Cook on LOW for 8 to 10 hours.

Before serving, turn the pork chops in the sauce again. Serve them with the extra sauce on the side.

YIELD: 4 servings

TIP: To make a great gravy, dissolve 3 tablespoons (24 g) flour in 1/2 cup (120 ml) water and add the mixture to the juices left in the slow cooker after the pork chops have been removed. Season the gravy with salt and freshly ground black pepper to taste.

ADD IT! Add 4 to 6 ounces (115 to 168 g) sliced fresh or canned mushrooms to the soup-and-wine mixture.

NUTRITIONAL ANALYSIS: One serving of the basic recipe (made with good white wine) contains 324 calories; 21 g fat; 24 g protein; 6 g carbohydrate; and .3 g dietary fiber.

DID YOU KNOW
Always use good-quality spirits when cooking. If you wouldn't want to drink it by the glass, you certainly don't want it smothering your pork chops.

Red Beans and Ham Hocks

Cooking time: 8 to 10 hours on LOW   5 to 6 hours on HIGH
Attention: Minimal

Grab a couple of slices of cornbread, some rice, and a seat at the picnic table under the old oak tree for a down-home meal of Red Beans and Ham Hocks. Can't you hear "What a Wonderful Life" playing in the distance?

Two 15-ounce (417-g) cans **red beans**, drained

1 1/2 cups (340 g) frozen **Seasoning-Blend Vegetables** (page 30), thawed

2 to 3 pounds (.9 to 1.4 kg) smoked **ham hocks**

Water

Salt and freshly ground black pepper

Put the red beans and Seasoning-Blend Vegetables in the slow cooker. Arrange the ham hocks on top of the beans and vegetables, then add enough water to cover everything. Cover and cook on LOW for 8 to 10 hours or on HIGH for 5 to 6 hours.

Before serving, stir the ham hocks, beans, and vegetables, and season the mixture with salt and pepper to taste.

YIELD: 10 servings

ADD IT! Put 1 clove garlic, minced, and 1 bay leaf along with the beans and vegetables.

NUTRITIONAL ANALYSIS: One serving of the basic recipe (made with 2 pounds smoked ham hocks) contains 559 calories; 18 g fat; 42 g protein; 58 g carbohydrate; and 24 g dietary fiber.

DID YOU KNOW
A ham hock is the lower part of a hog's hind leg.

Rosemary Lamb Stew

Cooking time: 6 to 8 hours on LOW   4 to 5 hours on HIGH
Attention: Minimal

The distinctive aroma of rosemary will scent the whole house. Great with garlic mashed potatoes and a green salad.

- 1 1/2 to 2 pounds (683 to 910 g) **lean lamb** or **lamb shanks**, cut into 1-inch (2.5-cm) cubes
- One 14-ounce (398-g) can **diced tomatoes** with green pepper and onion, undrained
- 1 1/2 teaspoons (9 g) salt
- 1/2 teaspoon freshly ground black pepper
- 1 sprig fresh **rosemary**

Spray the inside of the slow cooker with cooking spray.

Put the lamb cubes in the slow cooker and cover them with the diced tomatoes. Add the salt, pepper, and rosemary, and stir to combine. Cover and cook on LOW for 6 to 8 hours or on HIGH for 4 to 5 hours. (Cooking this stew on LOW, especially if using mutton, a less tender alternative to lamb, will bring out the best flavor.)

Before serving, remove the rosemary sprig.

YIELD: 6 servings

ADD IT! Add 4 medium potatoes, peeled and cut into 1-inch (2.5-cm) cubes, and 1/2 cup (61 g) baby carrots along with the lamb. Arrange the vegetables around the sides of the slow cooker to help them cook faster.

NUTRITIONAL ANALYSIS: One serving of the basic recipe (made with 1 1/2 pounds lean lamb) contains 250 calories; 19 g fat; 16 g protein; 4 g carbohydrate; and 1.2 g dietary fiber.

Venison Steak

Slow cooking makes venison moist and tender. Serve with wild rice and Ginger-Apricot Cranberry Sauce (page 97).

    3 pounds (1.4 kg) boneless shoulder-cut **venison steaks**

    1/2 cup (170 g) frozen **Seasoning-Blend Vegetables** (page 30), thawed

    One 10³/4-ounce (305-g) can condensed **cream of mushroom soup**

    1 soup can (306 ml) water

    1 teaspoon (6 g) salt

In a large skillet over medium heat, brown the venison steaks on both sides to render the fat; do not discard the fat. Drain the venison, then place it in the slow cooker.

Add the Seasoning-Blend Vegetables to the skillet and sauté them in the venison fat until the onion is translucent and all the vegetables are tender. Stir in the condensed soup, water, and salt, then pour the mixture over the venison steaks. Cover and cook on LOW for 8 to 10 hours, or until the venison steaks are tender. (Do not cook this dish on HIGH.)

YIELD: 12 servings

NUTRITIONAL ANALYSIS: One serving of the basic recipe contains 170 calories; 5 g fat; 27 g protein; 3 g carbohydrate; and .5 g dietary fiber.

DID YOU KNOW?

If you're having a hard time finding venison locally, or just want to learn more about it, go online to the Venison Forum, www.venison.com.

Chapter 11

• •

Main Dishes: Poultry

Chicken and turkey are so versatile and delicious! But nothing steals the fun from family dinners faster than sitting down to the same old poultry main dish night after night after night—except, perhaps, slaving over a hot stove. Get into a new groove! Explore the versatility of chicken and turkey, as well as Cornish game hen, using your slow cooker. Your family will enjoy the moist, delicious meals, and you'll appreciate the virtually care-free preparation.

🍲 Baked Whole Chicken

Cooking time: 6 to 8 hours   **Attention:** Minimal

A slow-baked chicken makes a nice presentation at the table. Not only does the chicken look festive on the platter, but its appetizing aroma announces that a special dinner is ready.

> 1 tablespoon (14 ml) **olive oil**
>
> 1 teaspoon **adobo seasoning**
>
> One 3- to 3 1/2-pound (1.4- to 1.6-kg) whole **chicken**, rinsed and dried inside and out

Put the olive oil and adobo seasoning in a small bowl and stir to combine. Spread the mixture evenly over the chicken, then place the chicken breast side up in the slow cooker. Cover and cook on LOW for 6 to 8 hours, or until the chicken is tender and the juices run clear.

Remove the chicken from the slow cooker using several spatulas or a meat fork, taking care to preserve the chicken's shape.

YIELD: 6 servings

TIP: To make a yummy gravy from the cooking liquid, dissolve 3 tablespoons (24 g) flour in 1/2 cup (120 ml) water and stir the mixture into the cooking liquid remaining in the slow cooker after the chicken has been removed. With the slow cooker on HIGH, cook and stir the mixture continuously until it thickens. Season the gravy with salt and freshly ground black pepper to taste.

ADD IT! Add 1/2 teaspoon Hungarian paprika to the olive oil along with the adobo seasoning. For a one-pot meal, put 4 potatoes, peeled and cubed, 1 cup (122 g) baby carrots, and 1/2 cup (120 ml) water in the bottom of the slow cooker, then place the prepared chicken on top of them. Increase the cooking time by about 1 hour, to ensure that the chicken is done and the vegetables are tender.

NUTRITIONAL ANALYSIS: One serving of the basic recipe (made with a 3-pound whole chicken) contains 355 calories; 26 g fat; 29 g protein; .5 g carbohydrate; and trace dietary fiber.

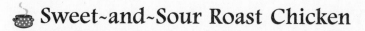 Sweet~and~Sour Roast Chicken

Cooking time: 6 to 8 hours

Attention: Remove cooking juices and add another ingredient during final hour

Carve up this sweet-and-sour taste treat. They'll think you spent an afternoon basting it to perfection. You won't need to mention that all you did was prepare the rice.

1 teaspoon **adobo seasoning**

One 10-ounce (280-g) jar **sweet-and-sour sauce**

One 3- to 4-pound (1.4- to 1.8-kg) whole **roasting chicken**, rinsed and dried inside and out

Put the adobo seasoning and 2 tablespoons (28 g) of the sweet-and-sour sauce in a small bowl and stir to combine. Brush the mixture evenly over the chicken, then place the chicken in the slow cooker. Cover and cook on LOW for 6 to 8 hours.

An hour before the chicken is done, remove most of the accumulated broth from the slow cooker using a bulb baster, leaving only enough to cover the bottom of the slow cooker. Pour the remaining sweet-and-sour sauce over the chicken and cook for 1 more hour, or until the sauce is bubbly and the chicken is fully cooked.

YIELD: 4 servings

NUTRITIONAL ANALYSIS: One serving of the basic recipe (made with a 3-pound whole roasting chicken) contains 808 calories; 39 g fat; 43 g protein; 69 g carbohydrate; and 2 g dietary fiber.

TRY THIS

Serve this rich dish with a luscious, refreshing fruit tea: Make unsweetened iced tea. Fill a pitcher 3/4 full with the tea, then top off with half orange juice and half apricot, peach, or mango nectar. Add slices of lemon and lime and serve over ice.

🍲 Coq au Vin

Cooking time: 6 to 8 hours on LOW   3 to 4 hours on HIGH
Attention: Minimal

What better way to prepare this traditional French dish than in the slow cooker? So simple, yet so full-flavored. Serve over egg noodles, with a slice of French bread.

  4 slices thickly cut **bacon**, cooked, drained, and crumbled

  One 3-pound (1.4-kg) whole **frying chicken**, cut into pieces

  2 cups (475 ml) wine-flavored **marinara sauce**

  Salt and freshly ground black pepper

Put the crumbled bacon in the slow cooker. Place the chicken pieces on top of the bacon and pour the marinara sauce over the chicken. Cover and cook on LOW for 6 to 8 hours or on HIGH for 3 to 4 hours, or until the chicken is thoroughly cooked.

Before serving, stir the chicken and sauce, and season them with salt and pepper to taste.

YIELD: 10 servings

ADD IT! In addition to the crumbled bacon, layer 1 cup (130 g) pearl onions, 1 cup (100 g) sliced mushrooms, and 1 clove garlic, minced, on the bottom of the slow cooker.

NUTRITIONAL ANALYSIS: One serving of the basic recipe contains 359 calories; 29 g fat; 19 g protein; 4 g carbohydrate; and .8 g dietary fiber.

TRY THIS

Don't forget the vin with your Coq au Vin! Buy a nice French red like a Bordeaux to add the perfect touch to this famous dish.

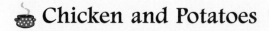 Chicken and Potatoes

Cooking time: 6 to 8 hours on LOW   3 to 4 hours on HIGH
Attention: Minimal

What a wonderful one-pot meal you'll have with only a few moments of preparation. Serve with biscuits and real creamery butter.

1/2 cup (175 ml) water

4 cups (480 g) frozen **stew vegetables** including potatoes, thawed

3 pounds (1.4 kg) bone-in **chicken pieces** with skin

1 teaspoon dried **basil**

1/2 teaspoon salt

1/2 teaspoon freshly ground black pepper

Pour the water into the slow cooker and add the stew vegetables. Place the chicken pieces on top of the stew vegetables, then sprinkle the chicken with the dried basil, salt, and pepper. Cover and cook on LOW for 6 to 8 hours or on HIGH for 3 to 4 hours.

YIELD: 6 servings

TIP: To make a yummy gravy from the cooking liquid, dissolve 3 tablespoons (24 g) flour in 1/2 cup (120 ml) water and stir the mixture into the cooking liquid remaining in the slow cooker after the chicken and vegetables have been removed. With the slow cooker on HIGH, cook and stir the mixture continuously until it thickens. Season the gravy with salt and freshly ground black pepper to taste.

ADD IT! Substitute chicken broth for the water.

NUTRITIONAL ANALYSIS: One serving of the basic recipe contains 412 calories; 24 g fat; 33 g protein; 17 g carbohydrate; and 5 g dietary fiber.

☕ Chicken Breasts Italian

Cooking time: 5 to 7 hours   **Attention:** Minimal

If you use your favorite bottled Italian dressing, you can't go wrong. And you won't waste any time either. Easy, quick, and *delicioso*!

> $^1/_2$ cup (175 ml) fat-free **Italian dressing**
>
> 6 bone-in **chicken breast halves**

Pour the Italian dressing into the slow cooker. Add the chicken breast halves and turn them to coat them with the dressing. Cover and cook on LOW for 5 to 7 hours, or until done.

YIELD: 6 servings

NUTRITIONAL ANALYSIS: One serving of the basic recipe contains 261 calories; 13 g fat; 30 g protein; 3 g carbohydrate; and 0 g dietary fiber.

IT'S GOOD FOR YOU

Serve this simple, healthy entrée with steamed spinach or broccoli and a fresh mixed-green salad with plenty of veggies for a super low-calorie meal. Or enjoy your spinach sautéed in oil with minced garlic for a heart-healthy treat.

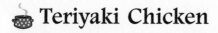 Teriyaki Chicken

Cooking time: 6 to 8 hours on LOW   3 to 4 hours on HIGH
Attention: Minimal

An Asian-style favorite. Serve over rice, topped with sauce, and accompanied by Asian-blend vegetables.

6 bone-in **chicken breast halves**

Two 16-ounce (455-g) cans **pineapple chunks**, one can drained and one can undrained

1 cup (288 ml) **teriyaki sauce**

Put the chicken breast halves in the slow cooker. In a large bowl, combine the pineapple chunks, pineapple juice, and teriyaki sauce, then pour the mixture over the chicken. Cover and cook on LOW for 6 to 8 hours or on HIGH for 3 to 4 hours, or until done.

YIELD: 6 servings

ADD IT! Substitute ¹/₂ cup (120 ml) white wine for ¹/₂ cup (120 ml) of the teriyaki sauce, and add 1 teaspoon minced garlic and ¹/₂ teaspoon minced fresh ginger. You can also add 8 ounces (225 g) fully cooked shrimp during the last hour of cooking. Continue cooking just until the shrimp are thoroughly warmed.

NUTRITIONAL ANALYSIS: One serving of the basic recipe contains 316 calories; 14 g fat; 33 g protein; 15 g carbohydrate; and .5 g dietary fiber.

IT'S GOOD FOR YOU

End your meal as they do in Chinese restaurants, with fresh fruit: orange slices, melon balls, and (of course) fresh pineapple. Refreshing and good for you!

Barbecued Chicken

Cooking time: 6 to 8 hours on LOW   3 to 4 hours on HIGH
Attention: Minimal

Serve over rice or on toasted rolls. The picnic table is optional.

- 3 pounds (1.4 kg) skinless, boneless **chicken breast halves**
- 2 cups (500 g) **barbecue sauce**
- 1 **onion**, chopped

Put the chicken breast halves in the slow cooker. In a medium-size bowl, combine the barbecue sauce and chopped onion, then pour the mixture over the chicken. Cover and cook on LOW for 6 to 8 hours or on HIGH for 3 to 4 hours, or until the chicken is thoroughly cooked.

YIELD: 10 generous servings

NUTRITIONAL ANALYSIS: One serving of the basic recipe contains 192 calories; 3 g fat; 33 g protein; 7 g carbohydrate; and .8 g dietary fiber.

TRY THIS

Serve up your barbecued chicken with traditional sides—hush puppies, cole slaw, and, for dessert, fresh peaches over vanilla ice cream. Don't forget the iced tea!

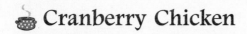 # Cranberry Chicken

Cooking time: 5 to 7 hours	**Attention**: Minimal

Cranberry Chicken is a refreshing twist on the usual weeknight fare. The sweet cranberry essence is enhanced by the tartness of the dressing.

> 1 1/2 pounds (683 g) skinless, boneless **chicken breast halves**
>
> One 16-ounce (455-g) can whole-berry or jellied **cranberry sauce**
>
> 1 cup (250 g) **French dressing**

Put the chicken breast halves in the slow cooker. In a medium-size bowl, combine the cranberry sauce and French dressing, then pour the mixture over the chicken. Cover and cook on LOW for 5 to 7 hours, or until the chicken is thoroughly cooked.

YIELD: 6 servings

ADD IT! Add a 2-ounce (55-g) envelope onion soup mix to the sauce-and-dressing mixture for a more complex flavor.

NUTRITIONAL ANALYSIS: One serving of the basic recipe contains 485 calories; 18 g fat; 44 g protein; 36 g carbohydrate; and .8 g dietary fiber.

IT'S GOOD FOR YOU

Cranberries are not only great sources of vitamin C, they're also packed with antioxidants, antibacterials, and antibiotics.

Chicken-Pizza Hot Dish

Cooking time: 6 to 8 1/2 hours on LOW   3 to 4 1/2 hours on HIGH
Attention: Stir and add more ingredients during final 5 to 10 minutes

Chicken on pizza—what a tasty combination. Serve this simple version over pasta, with a slice of garlic bread.

    8 skinless, boneless **chicken breast halves**

    2 cups (500 g) chunky-style **pasta sauce**

    Salt and freshly ground black pepper

    1 1/2 cups (168 g) **shredded pizza-blend cheese**

Put the chicken breast halves in the slow cooker and pour the pasta sauce over them. Cover and cook on LOW for 6 to 8 hours or on HIGH for 3 to 4 hours, or until the chicken is thoroughly cooked.

Stir the chicken and sauce, season them with salt and pepper to taste, and sprinkle them evenly with the shredded cheese. Cover and cook on LOW for an additional 5 to 10 minutes, or until the cheese has melted.

YIELD: 8 servings

NUTRITIONAL ANALYSIS: One serving of the basic recipe contains 198 calories; 7 g fat; 32 g protein; .5 g carbohydrate; and 0 g dietary fiber.

TRY THIS

Crank up the flavor by adding fresh or dried basil, thyme, and oregano to the sauce. Pour in some red wine (like Chianti) in the last half-hour of cooking to deepen the flavor. Serve with a crisp green salad with lots of raw veggies and a glass of red wine.

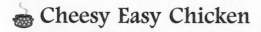 Cheesy Easy Chicken

Cooking time: 6 to 8 hours on LOW   3 to 4 hours on HIGH
Attention: Minimal

Chicken smothered in cheese sauce is a winning recipe, especially when it's so simple to fix. Serve with the cheese sauce ladled over steamed broccoli and cauliflower, and complement it with a basket of blueberry muffins.

> 2 pounds (910 g) skinless, boneless **chicken breast halves**
>
> One 10 3/4-ounce (305-g) can **condensed cream of chicken soup**
>
> One 10 3/4-ounce (305-g) can **condensed cheddar cheese soup**
>
> Salt and freshly ground black pepper

Put the chicken breast halves in the slow cooker. In a medium-size bowl, combine the condensed cream of chicken soup and condensed cheddar cheese soup, then pour the mixture over the chicken. Cover and cook on LOW for 6 to 8 hours or on HIGH for 3 to 4 hours, or until the chicken is thoroughly cooked.

Before serving, stir the chicken and sauce, and season them with salt and pepper to taste.

YIELD: 8 servings

ADD IT! Add 1 1/2 to 2 cups (150 to 200 g) cooked macaroni at the end of cooking and continue cooking until the macaroni is thoroughly heated.

NUTRITIONAL ANALYSIS: One serving of the basic recipe contains 193 calories; 6 g fat; 28 g protein; 5 g carbohydrate; and .4 g dietary fiber.

TRY THIS

Substitute a can of cream of tomato soup for the cream of chicken for a different but equally delicious flavor.

☕ Mandarin Chicken

Cooking time: 6 to 8 1/2 hours on LOW   3 to 4 1/2 hours on HIGH
Attention: Stir and add more ingredients during final 5 to 10 minutes

The addition of mandarin orange segments at the end of cooking sweetens this dish and adds eye appeal. Serve the chicken and sauce over hot rice, and garnish it with chopped green onion.

    2 pounds (910 g) skinless, boneless **chicken breast halves**

    One 11-ounce (310-g) can mandarin **orange segments**, undrained

    3/4 cup (175 ml) **Iron Chef Orange Sauce Glaze** with Ginger

    Salt and freshly ground black pepper

Put the chicken breast halves in the slow cooker. In a small bowl, combine the liquid from the canned mandarin orange segments and the glaze, then pour the mixture over the chicken. Cover and cook on LOW for 6 to 8 hours or on HIGH for 3 to 4 hours, or until the chicken is thoroughly cooked.

Stir the chicken and sauce, and season them with salt and pepper to taste. Add the mandarin orange segments and stir again. Cover and cook on LOW for an additional 5 to 10 minutes, or until the orange segments are thoroughly warmed.

YIELD: 8 servings

ADD IT! Add an 8-ounce (225-g) can water chestnuts, drained; an 8-ounce (225-g) can sliced mushrooms, drained; and 1 tablespoon (14 ml) soy sauce along with the liquid from the mandarin orange segments and the glaze.

NUTRITIONAL ANALYSIS: One serving of the basic recipe contains 144 calories; 2 g fat; 27 g protein; 5 g carbohydrate; and .3 g dietary fiber.

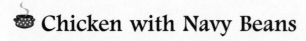 # Chicken with Navy Beans

Cooking time: 5 to 7 hours	**Attention:** Minimal

For a change of pace, try this delightful combination of chicken, navy beans, and tomatoes. Serve with French bread and herbed butter.

6 skinless, boneless **chicken breast halves**

One 15-ounce (417-g) can **navy beans**, drained and rinsed

One 14-ounce (398-g) can **diced tomatoes** with balsamic vinegar, basil, and olive oil, undrained

$^1/_2$ teaspoon salt

$^1/_4$ teaspoon freshly ground black pepper

Put the chicken breast halves in the slow cooker. In a large bowl, combine the navy beans, diced tomatoes, salt, and pepper, then pour the mixture over the chicken. Cover and cook on LOW for 5 to 7 hours, or until the chicken is thoroughly cooked.

Serve the chicken on a warm platter, topped with the beans and sauce.

YIELD: 6 servings

NUTRITIONAL ANALYSIS: One serving of the basic recipe contains 227 calories; 2 g fat; 34 g protein; 18 g carbohydrate; and 5 g dietary fiber.

DID YOU KNOW?

Navy beans are about the size of peas. Notwithstanding their diminutive size, navy beans are interchangeable with other white beans, so feel free to substitute Great Northern or cannelloni beans for navy beans in any recipe.

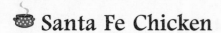 Santa Fe Chicken

Cooking time: 5 to 7 hours on LOW 2 1/2 to 3 1/2 hours on HIGH
Attention: Minimal

This simple version of a favorite southwestern dish goes well with Cuban bread, butter, and a green salad.

> Two 15-ounce (417-g) cans **Mexican corn** with red and green peppers
>
> 1 cup (225 g) **chunky-style salsa**
>
> 6 skinless, boneless **chicken breast halves**

Put the corn and 1/2 cup (113 g) of the salsa in the slow cooker and stir to combine. Place the chicken breast halves on top of the corn-salsa mixture, then pour the remaining salsa over the chicken. Cover and cook on LOW for 5 to 7 hours or on HIGH for 2 1/2 to 3 1/2 hours, or until the chicken is tender.

Serve the chicken from the slow cooker for an easy cleanup.

YIELD: 6 servings

ADD IT! Add a 15-ounce (417-g) can black beans, rinsed and drained, along with the corn. When the chicken is done, sprinkle it with 1 cup (115 g) shredded Mexican-blend cheese, cover, and cook on LOW for an additional 10 minutes, or until the cheese has melted.

NUTRITIONAL ANALYSIS: One serving of the basic recipe contains 265 calories; 5 g fat; 31 g protein; 27 g carbohydrate; and 3 g dietary fiber.

TRY THIS

Serve this colorful dish in bright Fiestaware or earthenware dishes with colorful napkins and placemats. Add some margaritas or Mexican beer like Dos Equis. Ole!

 Chicken Adobo

Cooking time: 6 to 8 hours   **Attention:** Minimal

You can dress up this versatile main dish or keep it simple. Feel free to use chicken thighs, breasts, or mixed light and dark meat. Any way you fix it, Chicken Adobo tastes fabulous, and it couldn't be easier to prepare.

> 2 pounds (910 g) bone-in **chicken thighs** with skin, browned in 1 tablespoon (14 ml) vegetable oil, if desired
>
> 1 cup (235 ml) water
>
> 1/2 cup (120 ml) **apple cider vinegar**
>
> 1/4 cup (60 ml) **soy sauce**
>
> 1 teaspoon freshly ground black pepper

Put the chicken thighs in the slow cooker. In a medium-size bowl, combine the water, apple cider vinegar, soy sauce, and pepper, then pour the mixture over the chicken. Turn the chicken thighs to coat them with the sauce. Cover and cook on LOW for 6 to 8 hours.

YIELD: 4 generous servings

ADD IT! If you like the taste of garlic, substitute garlic-flavored soy sauce for the plain soy sauce. If you don't have this gourmet soy sauce on hand, add 2 cloves garlic, minced, to the marinade along with the plain soy sauce. For an authentic touch, substitute coconut milk for the water.

NUTRITIONAL ANALYSIS: One serving of the basic recipe contains 424 calories; 31 g fat; 32 g protein; 4 g carbohydrate; and .3 g dietary fiber.

TRY THIS

Serve on soft flour tortillas with a side of refried beans.

 Italian Chicken

Cooking time: 6 to 8 hours on LOW   3 to 4 hours on HIGH
Attention: Minimal

Mama mia! Prepared pasta sauce makes this main dish a snap. Serve over whole-wheat pasta or on a toasted roll, and add a green salad for a healthful treat.

1 to 1 1/2 pounds (455 to 683 g) bone-in **chicken thighs**, skin removed

One 32-ounce (905-g) jar chunky-style **pasta sauce** with mushrooms

1 teaspoon (.8 g) **Italian Seasoning** (page 29)

1/4 teaspoon freshly ground black pepper

Put the chicken thighs in the slow cooker. In a large bowl, combine the pasta sauce, Italian Seasoning, and pepper, then pour the mixture over the chicken. Cover and cook on LOW for 6 to 8 hours or on HIGH for 3 to 4 hours, or until the chicken is thoroughly cooked.

YIELD: 4 generous servings

NUTRITIONAL ANALYSIS: One serving of the basic recipe (made with 1 pound chicken thighs) contains 78 calories; 3 g fat; 13 g protein; .3 g carbohydrate; and trace dietary fiber.

IT'S GOOD FOR YOU

For extra texture, vitamins, minerals, and protein, add sliced fresh mushrooms and chopped green bell peppers in the last half-hour of cooking. Serve over steamed spaghetti squash for a healthy high-fiber, low-carb dish.

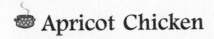 Apricot Chicken

Cooking time: 6 to 8 hours on LOW   3 to 4 hours on HIGH
Attention: Minimal

A sweet-and-sour chicken recipe in which apricots make all the difference.
Serve with a salad of mixed baby greens and lemon–poppy seed muffins.

8 bone-in **chicken thighs**, skin removed

One 2-ounce (55-g) envelope **onion soup mix**

One to two 12-ounce (355-ml) cans **apricot nectar**

Put the chicken thighs in the slow cooker. Sprinkle the chicken thighs with the soup mix, then pour enough apricot nectar into the slow cooker to cover them. Cover and cook on LOW for 6 to 8 hours or on HIGH for 3 to 4 hours, or until the chicken is thoroughly cooked.

YIELD: 8 servings

NUTRITIONAL ANALYSIS: One serving of the basic recipe (made with 1 can apricot nectar) contains 127 calories; 3 g fat; 15 g protein; 10 g carbohydrate; and 1 g dietary fiber.

TRY THIS

Carry the apricot theme through your meal by adding sliced fresh or dried apricots and slivered almonds to the salad and substituting apricot-cranberry muffins for the lemon-poppy seed muffins.

🍲 Peachy Chicken

Cooking time: 5 to 7 hours on LOW   2 1/2 to 3 1/2 hours on HIGH
Attention: Minimal

This light, refreshing chicken dish is delicious over angel hair pasta. Serve with summer squash and a crusty baguette with herbed butter.

4 skinless, boneless **chicken thighs**

1/2 cup (160 g) **peach preserves**

2 tablespoons (28 ml) water

1/2 teaspoon **dried basil**

Salt and freshly ground black pepper

Put the chicken thighs in the slow cooker. In a small bowl, combine the peach preserves, water, and dried basil, then pour the mixture over the chicken. Cover and cook on LOW for 5 to 7 hours or on HIGH for 2 1/2 to 3 1/2 hours, or until the chicken is thoroughly cooked.

Before serving, stir the chicken and sauce, and season them with salt and pepper to taste.

YIELD: 4 servings

NUTRITIONAL ANALYSIS: One serving of the basic recipe contains 180 calories; 3 g fat; 14 g protein; 26 g carbohydrate; and .5 g dietary fiber.

TRY THIS

Substitute your favorite preserves to give this dish a different delicious flavor. Try cherry or apricot preserves, red currant or apple cider jelly, orange or ginger marmalade, or even a fruit chutney.

 Hot Barbecued Chicken Wings

Cooking time: 6 to 8 hours on LOW   3 to 4 hours on HIGH
Attention: Minimal

Everybody loves barbecue hot wings. Who knew they could be this easy to make? Serve as an appetizer, with celery and blue cheese dressing, or add fried potatoes and a green salad for a full meal.

5 pounds (2.3 kg) **chicken wings**, with or without the tips cut off

One 16-ounce (455-g) bottle **barbecue sauce**

1/4 teaspoon **hot pepper sauce**

Put the chicken wings in the slow cooker. In a medium-size bowl, combine the barbecue sauce and hot pepper sauce, then pour the mixture over the chicken wings. Cover and cook on LOW for 6 to 8 hours or on HIGH for 3 to 4 hours.

YIELD: 8 servings

NUTRITIONAL ANALYSIS: One serving of the basic recipe contains 383 calories; 26 g fat; 29 g protein; 7 g carbohydrate; and .6 g dietary fiber.

TRY THIS

Not a wings fan? You can substitute 5 pounds of chicken thighs, breasts, pre-made meatballs, or even sliced hot dogs if you prefer.

Lemon, Rosemary, and Garlic Chicken

Cooking time: 5 to 7 hours on LOW   2 1/2 to 3 1/2 hours on HIGH
Attention: Minimal

This scrumptious chicken dish gets its sparkle from a bit o' the bubbly. Serve over rice, with a crusty loaf of focaccia bread and olive-oil dipping sauce.

  2 pounds (910 g) skinless, **boneless chicken breasts**, cut into chunks of uniform size

  3/4 cup (175 ml) **Emeril Lemon, Rosemary, and Garlic Marinade**

  3/4 cup (175 ml) **lemon-lime soda**

Put the chicken chunks in the slow cooker. In a small bowl, combine the marinade and lemon-lime soda, then pour the mixture over the chicken. Cover and cook on LOW for 5 to 7 hours or on HIGH for 2 1/2 to 3 1/2 hours, or until the chicken is thoroughly cooked.

YIELD: 8 servings

TIP: If you use frozen chicken breasts for this recipe, partially thaw them in the microwave. When they're a smidgeon away from being completely thawed, cut them into chunks using a sharp knife. You'll be pleasantly surprised by how much easier it is to cut chicken that's still slightly firm from being frozen. Don't forget to finish thawing the chunks in the microwave or in cold water, if necessary, before placing them in the slow cooker. If you use fresh chicken, place the breasts in the freezer for 10 to 15 minutes to enjoy the same cutting ease.

NUTRITIONAL ANALYSIS: One serving of the basic recipe contains 138 calories; 1.9 g fat; 27 g protein; 1.9 g carbohydrate; and .4 g dietary fiber.

TRY THIS

Make your own dipping sauce by infusing sprigs of rosemary, thyme, and/or fresh basil in olive oil overnight.

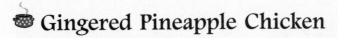 Gingered Pineapple Chicken

Cooking time: 5 to 7 hours   **Attention:** Minimal

Fresh ginger provides a little zing. Spoon the pineapple-ginger sauce over the chicken and rice. Serve with steamed asparagus.

> One 16-ounce (455-g) can **sweet-and-sour sauce** with pineapple
>
> 1 tablespoon (6 g) minced fresh **ginger**
>
> 1/2 teaspoon salt
>
> 1/4 teaspoon freshly ground black pepper
>
> 6 skinless, boneless **chicken breast halves**, cut into cubes

Put the sweet-and-sour sauce, minced ginger, salt, and pepper in the slow cooker and stir to combine. Add the chicken cubes and stir again. Cover and cook on LOW for 5 to 7 hours, or until the chicken is thoroughly cooked.

Serve the chicken and sauce over rice.

YIELD: 6 servings

ADD IT! Add 2 cloves garlic, minced, to the sauce. Garnish the chicken with sliced green onion.

NUTRITIONAL ANALYSIS: One serving of the basic recipe contains 425 calories; 2 g fat; 28 g protein; 73 g carbohydrate; and 2 g dietary fiber.

TRY THIS

Serve this dish with ginger ale, or a punch made from equal parts ginger ale, pineapple juice, and cranberry juice.

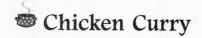 Chicken Curry

In the mood for a romantic dinner for two? Then you're in the mood for quick-and-easy Chicken Curry. Garnish with chopped green onion, and serve with brown rice and hot Indian bread.

> 2 skinless, boneless **chicken breast halves**, cut into strips
>
> 1 cup (225 g) **curry sauce**

Put the chicken strips and curry sauce in the slow cooker and stir to combine. Cook on LOW for 3 to 4 1/2 hours, or until the chicken strips are thoroughly cooked.

YIELD: 2 servings

NUTRITIONAL ANALYSIS: One serving of the basic recipe contains 191 calories; 5 g fat; 29 g protein; 7 g carbohydrate; and 0 g dietary fiber.

DID YOU KNOW?

For an authentic accompaniment, serve an Indian flatbread such as chapati or nan. Supermarkets are starting to carry Indian bread, but if yours doesn't, you can find it at an Indian grocery store.

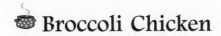 Broccoli Chicken

Cooking time: 3 to 4 hours
Attention: Add more ingredients during final hour

A perennial favorite, this creamy broccoli-and-chicken meal tastes especially yummy served over rice and with homemade biscuits and honey.

> 2 pounds (910 g) fully cooked skinless, **boneless chicken breasts**, cut into bite-size pieces
>
> One 10¾-ounce (305-g) can **condensed cream of broccoli soup**
>
> ¾ cup (175 ml) **milk**
>
> Salt and freshly ground black pepper

Put the chicken pieces and condensed soup in the slow cooker and mix well. Cover and cook on LOW for 2 to 3 hours.

Add the milk and stir. Season the mixture with salt and pepper to taste and stir again. Cover and cook for 1 more hour, or until the mixture is thoroughly heated.

YIELD: 8 servings

ADD IT! Add 2 cups (140 g) broccoli florets, steamed, during the last half hour of cooking.

NUTRITIONAL ANALYSIS: One serving of the basic recipe contains 217 calories; 9 g fat; 29 g protein; 4 g carbohydrate; and .1 g dietary fiber.

IT'S GOOD FOR YOU

Broccoli has been acclaimed as the healthiest veggie of all. It's packed with vitamin C, vitamin A, calcium, and fiber. But it's most renowned for its cancer-fighting compounds.

Cornish Game Hens and Wild Rice

Cooking time: 6 to 8 hours   **Attention:** Minimal

These small hens are succulent and tender, and the wild rice is the perfect complement. Serve with Marmalade-Glazed Carrots (page 204) and crusty bread.

> One 6-ounce (168-g) envelope **wild rice and long-grain converted rice mix**
>
> 1 1/2 cups (355 ml) **water**
>
> 2 Cornish **game hens**
>
> 1/2 teaspoon salt
>
> 1/4 teaspoon freshly ground black pepper

Put the rice mix and water in the slow cooker and stir to combine. Place the Cornish game hens on top of the rice mixture and sprinkle them with the salt and pepper. Cover and cook on LOW for 6 to 8 hours, or until the hens are thoroughly cooked and the rice is tender.

YIELD: 2 generous servings

NUTRITIONAL ANALYSIS: One serving of the basic recipe contains 977 calories; 48 g fat; 70 g protein; 64 g carbohydrate; and 6 g dietary fiber.

TRY THIS

Can't find Cornish game hens? You can substitute four quail or one chicken in this recipe, and the results will still be delicious!

Cornish Game Hens in Wine Sauce

Cooking time: 6 to 8 hours on LOW   3 to 4 hours on HIGH

Attention: Minimal.

For a change of pace, try Cornish game hen in place of chicken. Serve this elegant dish over rice or noodles and accompanied by Italian bread. Yummy!

- 3 Cornish **game hens**, cut in half lengthwise
- ¹/₂ cup (120 ml) **dry sherry**
- 1 teaspoon **Italian Seasoning** (page 29)
- Salt and freshly ground black pepper

Put the Cornish game hen halves in the slow cooker. Pour the dry sherry over the hens, then sprinkle the hens with the Italian Seasoning and salt and pepper to taste. Cover and cook on LOW for 6 to 8 hours or on HIGH for 3 to 4 hours, or until the hens are thoroughly cooked and the juices run clear.

YIELD: 6 servings

ADD IT! Place the hens on top of 1 medium onion, chopped. Add ¹/₂ cup (50 g) sliced fresh mushrooms along with the sherry.

NUTRITIONAL ANALYSIS: One serving of the basic recipe contains 359 calories; 24 g fat; 29 g protein; 1 g carbohydrate; and trace dietary fiber.

DID YOU KNOW?

A Cornish game hen is actually a small breed of chicken, a cross between the Cornish and White Rock breeds, which mature at about 21/2 pounds each.

🍲 Turkey Breast with Gravy

Cooking time: 8 to 10 hours	**Attention:** Minimal

Slow cooking a turkey breast will provide the wonderful aroma you've come to expect from a holiday meal. Enjoy this moist and tender turkey with gravy, mashed potatoes, and a green vegetable.

One 2-pound (910-g) **turkey breast**, or a size that fits inside your covered slow cooker

One 12-ounce (340-g) jar **turkey gravy**

2 cloves **garlic**, minced

Put the turkey breast in the slow cooker. In a small bowl, combine the turkey gravy and minced garlic, then pour the mixture over the turkey. Cover and cook on LOW for 8 to 10 hours, or until the turkey is thoroughly cooked.

Remove the turkey from the slow cooker, place it on a platter, and let it rest for 10 minutes. Serve it with the extra gravy on the side.

YIELD: 8 servings

ADD IT! Substitute 1 1/2 cups (285 ml) dry white wine mixed with two .9-ounce (25-g) envelopes chicken-and-herb gravy mix for the jar of turkey gravy.

NUTRITIONAL ANALYSIS: One serving of the basic recipe contains 149 calories; 2 g fat; 29 g protein; 2 g carbohydrate; and .1 g dietary fiber.

TRY THIS

If you have leftovers, serve them over toast for a delicious hot lunch.

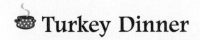 Turkey Dinner

Cooking time: 8 to 10 hours on LOW   4 to 5 hours on HIGH
Attention: Minimal

It's so simple and quick to make a one-pot turkey meal. Thicken the gravy, if you wish, and enjoy it with the turkey, vegetables, and biscuits.

4 cups (480 g) frozen **stew vegetables**, thawed

2 pounds (910 g) bone-in **turkey thighs**, skin removed

One 10³/₄-ounce can (305-g) **condensed cream of mushroom soup**

¹/₄ cup (60 ml) water

Put the stew vegetables in the bottom of the slow cooker and place the turkey thighs on top of them. In a small bowl, combine the condensed soup and water, then pour the mixture over the turkey and vegetables. Cover and cook on LOW for 8 to 10 hours or on HIGH for 4 to 5 hours, or until the turkey is thoroughly cooked and the vegetables are tender.

YIELD: 8 generous servings

ADD IT! Add 1 medium onion, chopped, and 2 cloves garlic, minced, to the soup mixture, and substitute sherry for the water.

NUTRITIONAL ANALYSIS: One serving of the basic recipe contains 332 calories; 14 g fat; 35 g protein; 15 g carbohydrate; and 4 g dietary fiber.

TRY THIS

Don't forget the cranberry sauce! Try the Ginger-Apricot-Cranberry Sauce on page 97.

🍲 Broccoli, Rice, and Turkey

This flavorful one-pot meal pleases with so little effort. A perfect follow-up meal after a holiday stint in the kitchen. Serve with steamed broccoli and dinner rolls.

- 1 1/4 cups (231 g) raw **converted rice**
- 1/4 teaspoon freshly ground black pepper
- 2 pounds (910 g) skinless, **boneless turkey breast**, cut into strips
- 1 1/2 cups (355 ml) hot water
- One 3-ounce (85-g) envelope **cream of broccoli soup mix**

Spray the inside of the slow cooker with cooking spray.

Put the raw rice in the slow cooker, sprinkle it with the pepper, and top it with the turkey strips. In a medium-size bowl, combine the hot water and soup mix, then pour the mixture over the rice and turkey strips. Cover and cook on LOW for 6 to 8 hours, or until the turkey strips are thoroughly cooked and the rice is tender.

YIELD: 8 servings

TIP: If you're using fresh turkey breast for this recipe, use this trick to make slicing it quick and easy. Place the turkey breast in the freezer for 10 to 15 minutes, until ice crystals just start to form on the surface of the meat. Remove the meat from the freezer and cut it into strips using a sharp knife. Don't forget to thaw the strips in cold water, if necessary, before placing them in the slow cooker.

NUTRITIONAL ANALYSIS: One serving of the basic recipe contains 243 calories; 1 g fat; 30 g protein; 25 g carbohydrate; and .5 g dietary fiber.

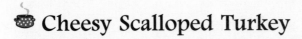 Cheesy Scalloped Turkey

Cooking time: 5 to 7 hours on LOW   2 1/2 to 3 1/2 hours on HIGH
Attention: Minimal

Another holiday-meal follow-up dish. Cheesy potatoes make this one a welcome reprise.

  2 cups (475 ml) water
  One 5-ounce (140-g) package **cheesy scalloped potatoes and seasoning mix**
  One 1-pound (455-g) fully cooked skinless, **boneless turkey breast**, cut into strips
  One 10-ounce (280-g) package **frozen peas**

Put the water and the contents of the scalloped potatoes kit, including the seasoning mix, in the slow cooker and stir to combine. Add the turkey strips and frozen peas, and stir again. Cover and cook on LOW for 5 to 7 hours or on HIGH for 2 1/2 to 3 1/2 hours.

YIELD: 4 servings

NUTRITIONAL ANALYSIS: One serving of the basic recipe contains 391 calories; 10 g fat; 39 g protein; 36 g carbohydrate; and 8 g dietary fiber.

DID YOU KNOW?

Scalloped potatoes don't get their name from their resemblance to seafood! Instead, scalloping refers to the technique of cooking potato slices in milk.

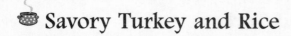 Savory Turkey and Rice

Cooking time: 6 to 8 hours on LOW   3 to 4 hours on HIGH
Attention: Minimal

One-pot dishes are fabulous for those days when you're pushed for time. A basket of flaky biscuits or crusty bread is all you need for a lovely meal.

- 2 cups (350 g) chopped **cooked turkey**
- One 14-ounce (398-g) can **diced tomatoes** with garlic, oregano, and basil, undrained
- 1 cup (235 ml) water
- 3/4 cup (139 g) **raw converted rice**
- Salt and freshly ground black pepper

Put the chopped cooked turkey, diced tomatoes, water, and raw rice in the slow cooker and stir to combine. Cover and cook on LOW for 6 to 8 hours or on HIGH for 3 to 4 hours.

Before serving, stir the turkey mixture and season it with salt and pepper to taste.

YIELD: 8 servings

ADD IT! Add 1 1/2 cups (340 g) frozen Seasoning-Blend Vegetables (page 30), 1/2 cup (120 ml) sherry, and 2 cloves garlic, minced.

NUTRITIONAL ANALYSIS: One serving of the basic recipe contains 135 calories; 2 g fat; 12 g protein; 16 g carbohydrate; and 1 g dietary fiber.

TRY THIS

You can turn this dish into a nourishing and filling soup by adding two cans of turkey or chicken broth to the cooker.

Chapter 12

• •

Main Dishes: Fish and Shellfish

Fish and shellfish are naturally tender and flavorful. They are a fabulous source of lean protein and other important nutrients, so two servings a week are recommended. Zesty Citrus Catfish (page 160), Wine-Poached Salmon (page 164), and Shrimp and Mushroom Marinara (page 169) are just some of the tasty slow-cooker recipes you can use to tempt your taste buds to eat right. Employ your slow cooker in the pursuit of exceptional health!

🍃 Zesty Citrus Catfish

Lime is the twist in this zesty dish. Serve with parsleyed new potatoes and a salad of spring-mix greens.

1 cup (235 ml) **chicken broth**

1/2 cup (120 ml) **Lawry's Tequila Lime Marinade**

1 1/2 pounds (683 g) **catfish fillets** of uniform thickness

Salt and freshly ground black pepper

Spray the inside of the slow cooker with cooking spray.

Put the chicken broth and marinade in the slow cooker and stir to combine. Arrange the catfish fillets skin sides down in the broth-marinade mixture. Cover and cook on LOW for 2 to 3 hours, or until the fish can easily be flaked with a fork.

Before serving, season the catfish with salt and pepper to taste.

YIELD: 6 servings

NUTRITIONAL ANALYSIS: One serving of the basic recipe contains 177 calories; 10 g fat; 20 g protein; 1 g carbohydrate; and trace dietary fiber.

IT'S GOOD FOR YOU

Spring mix, also called field greens or mesclun, is becoming all the rage for the health-conscious. Originating in France, spring mix consists of tender young leaves from a variety of plants, as well as edible flowers upon occasion. The bags of prewashed spring mix found at your local grocer are likely to include endive, radicchio, sorrel, frissee, chervil, and other highly nutritious greens, but probably not the edible flowers.

 Lemon~Poached Salmon

Cooking time: 3 to 4 hours on LOW   1 1/2 to 2 hours on HIGH
Attention: Minimal

Slow cooking brings out the flavor in Lemon-Poached Salmon. Serve with garlic mashed potatoes and a green vegetable.

1 cup (235 ml) **chicken broth**

1 1/4 pounds (569 g) **salmon fillets** of uniform thickness

1/2 teaspoon salt

1/4 teaspoon freshly ground black pepper

1/2 **lemon**, cut into thin slices

Spray the inside of the slow cooker with cooking spray.

Pour the chicken broth into the slow cooker, then arrange the salmon fillets skin sides down in one layer in the broth. Season the fillets with the salt and pepper, and place the lemon slices on top of them. Cover and cook on LOW for 3 to 4 hours or on HIGH for 1 1/2 to 2 hours, or until the salmon can easily be flaked with a fork.

YIELD: 4 servings

ADD IT! Substitute white wine for half the chicken broth, and sprinkle a mixture of 1/2 cup (65 g) chopped onion, 1/2 cup (60 g) chopped celery, and 1 clove garlic, minced, around the fillets.

NUTRITIONAL ANALYSIS: One serving of the basic recipe contains 175 calories; 5 g fat; 30 g protein; .3 g carbohydrate; and trace dietary fiber.

Orange Salmon

Cooking time: 3 to 4 hours on LOW   1 1/2 to 2 hours on HIGH
Attention: Minimal

The subtle infusion of orange and ginger gives this salmon dish a fresh flavor that's perfect for company. Garnish with chopped green onion, and serve with fluffy rice and steamed snow peas.

   1 pound (455 g) **salmon fillets** of uniform thickness

   3/4 cup (175 ml) **Iron Chef Orange Sauce Glaze** with Ginger

   1/4 cup (60 ml) **vegetable** or **chicken broth**

Spray the inside of the slow cooker with cooking spray.

Arrange the salmon fillets skin sides down in one layer in the bottom of the slow cooker. In a small bowl, combine the glaze and broth, then pour the mixture over the fillets. Cover and cook on LOW for 3 to 4 hours or on HIGH for 1 1/2 to 2 hours, or until the salmon can easily be flaked with a fork.

YIELD: 4 servings

ADD IT! For salmon with a zing, add 1/2 teaspoon grated fresh ginger to the glaze-broth mixture.

NUTRITIONAL ANALYSIS: One serving of the basic recipe (made with vegetable broth) contains 172 calories; 4 g fat; 24 g protein; 8 g carbohydrate; and .3 g dietary fiber.

TRY THIS

Just for fun, add touches of orange throughout the meal. Make a fresh green salad with Mandarin orange slices and slivered almonds and top with an orange vinaigrette. Serve a white cake with orange frosting for dessert.

Teriyaki Salmon

Cooking time: 3 to 4 hours on LOW   1 1/2 to 2 hours on HIGH
Attention: Minimal

The tasty teriyaki sauce made with this dish is also good over hot, buttered rice. Add a salad of baby greens, and you're all set for dinner.

3/4 cup (175 ml) **apple cider**

1/4 cup (60 ml) **teriyaki sauce**

1 1/4 pounds (569 g) **salmon fillets** of uniform thickness

1/2 teaspoon salt

Spray the inside of the slow cooker with cooking spray.

Put the apple cider and teriyaki sauce in the slow cooker and stir to combine. Arrange the salmon fillets skin sides down in one layer in the apple cider–teriyaki sauce mixture, then sprinkle the fillets with the salt. Cover and cook on LOW for 3 to 4 hours or on HIGH for 1 1/2 to 2 hours, or until the salmon can easily be flaked with a fork.

YIELD: 4 servings

ADD IT! Add 1 to 2 teaspoons (3 to 7 g) minced garlic to the sauce mixture. Garnish the salmon with chopped green onion.

NUTRITIONAL ANALYSIS: One serving of the basic recipe contains 202 calories; 5 g fat; 29 g protein; 8 g carbohydrate; and trace dietary fiber.

TRY THIS
Pass the fortune cookies after dinner!

Wine-Poached Salmon

Cooking time: 3 to 4 hours on LOW   1 1/2 to 2 hours on HIGH
Attention: Minimal

This classic salmon preparation is as delicious as it's healthful. Serve with Hollandaise sauce, if desired, and add Maple-Glazed Baby Carrots (page 203) and potato sourdough rolls to round out the menu.

1 pound (455 g) **salmon fillets** of uniform size and thickness

1/2 teaspoon salt

1/4 teaspoon freshly ground black pepper

6 ounces (175 ml) **white wine**

6 ounces (175 ml) water

1 teaspoon dried **bouquet garni**, bundled in cheesecloth

Spray the inside of the slow cooker with cooking spray.

Arrange the salmon fillets in one layer in the bottom of the slow cooker and sprinkle them with the salt and pepper. In a small bowl, combine the white wine and water, then pour the mixture over the fillets. Add the bouquet garni, allowing it to float in the wine mixture. Cover and cook on LOW for 3 to 4 hours or on HIGH for 1 1/2 to 2 hours, or until the salmon can easily be flaked with a fork.

Before serving, remove the bouquet garni.

YIELD: 4 servings

NUTRITIONAL ANALYSIS: One serving of the basic recipe contains 161 calories; 4 g fat; 23 g protein; .5 g carbohydrate; and trace dietary fiber.

IT'S GOOD FOR YOU
Bouquet garni is a mixture of herbs, either fresh or dried. It's used to enhance the flavor of soups, stews, and sauces. You can find dried bouquet garni in the spice aisle of your supermarket, or you can make your own fresh bouquet garni by tying together 3 sprigs of fresh parsley, 1 sprig of fresh thyme, and 1 bay leaf. Use clean kitchen string to bundle them so that you can easily remove them before serving your meal.

🐟 Au Gratin Salmon and Potato Bake

Cooking time: 4 1/2 to 5 1/2 hours   **Attention:** Minimal

The marriage of salmon and potatoes is comfort food at its best. Serve with corn-on-the-cob and whole-wheat rolls.

One 19-ounce (540-g) bag frozen **Green Giant Au Gratin Potatoes**

One 14 1/2-ounce (419-g) can **Alaskan salmon**, drained and flaked

One 10 3/4-ounce (305-g) can **condensed cream of celery soup**

Spray the inside of the slow cooker with cooking spray.

Put the frozen potatoes in the slow cooker and spread them out evenly. Top the potatoes with the salmon, then pour the condensed soup over the potatoes. Cover and cook on HIGH for 4 1/2 to 5 1/2 hours, or until the potatoes are fork-tender.

YIELD: 5 servings

NUTRITIONAL ANALYSIS: One serving of the basic recipe contains 245 calories; 11 g fat; 20 g protein; 15 g carbohydrate; and 2 g dietary fiber.

IT'S GOOD FOR YOU

Always choose wild Alaskan salmon over farmed salmon. Wild salmon is an important source of heart-healthy omega-3 fats and vitamin E. More important, it's harvested from the pristine waters of Alaska, where it matured untouched by antibiotics, pesticides, growth hormones, and synthetic coloring agents.

White Beans with Tuna

Cooking time: 5 1/2 to 7 1/2 hours on LOW   3 to 4 hours on HIGH
Attention: Change heat setting and add another ingredient during final 30 minutes

Traditionally served cold, this summer favorite can be just as yummy hot from the slow cooker. Serve with crusty French bread slathered with melted basil-garlic butter (see "Try This," below).

2 cups (500 g) olive oil, garlic, and tomato–flavored **pasta sauce**

One 16-ounce (455-g) can **white beans**, rinsed and drained

Two 12-ounce (340-g) cans **tuna**, drained and flaked

Salt and freshly ground black pepper

Put the pasta sauce and white beans in the slow cooker and stir to combine. Cover and cook on LOW for 5 to 7 hours or on HIGH for 2 1/2 to 3 1/2 hours.

Add the flaked tuna and stir. Cover and cook on HIGH for an additional 30 minutes.

Before serving, stir the mixture again and season it with salt and pepper to taste.

YIELD: 8 servings

NUTRITIONAL ANALYSIS: One serving of the basic recipe contains 165 calories; .9 g fat; 26 g protein; 13 g carbohydrate; and 3 g dietary fiber.

TRY THIS
To make basil-garlic butter, combine 8 tablespoons (1 stick, or 112 g) butter, softened, 3 tablespoons (7.5 g) finely chopped fresh basil or 1 teaspoon dried basil, 2 teaspoons (7 g) finely minced garlic, and 1 teaspoon lemon juice.

 Tuna Casserole

Cooking time: 5 to 6 hours on LOW   2 1/2 to 3 hours on HIGH
Attention: Minimal

A perennial favorite, Tuna Casserole is ready for the table after a scant few minutes of preparation in the morning. Serve over egg noodles or rice—and don't forget the basket of flaky buttermilk biscuits.

> Two 10 3/4-ounce (305-g) cans **condensed cream of chicken soup**
>
> One 10-ounce (280-g) bag **frozen peas and carrots**, thawed
>
> Three 6 1/2-ounce (183-g) cans **tuna**, drained and flaked
>
> Salt and freshly ground black pepper

Put the condensed soup and thawed peas and carrots in the slow cooker and stir to combine. Add the flaked tuna and stir again gently. Cover and cook on LOW for 5 to 6 hours or on HIGH for 2 1/2 to 3 hours.

Before serving, stir the casserole and season it with salt and pepper to taste.

YIELD: 6 generous servings

ADD IT! Add 1 cup (235 ml) evaporated milk to the soup mixture. An hour before the casserole is done, stir in 8 ounces (225 g) uncooked egg noodles and 3 hard-boiled eggs, chopped; cook until the egg noodles are tender.

NUTRITIONAL ANALYSIS: One serving of the basic recipe contains 210 calories; 6 g fat; 27 g protein; 12 g carbohydrate; and 2 g dietary fiber.

IT'S GOOD FOR YOU

Tuna is an excellent source of lean protein. It's also low in saturated fats and cholesterol.

Seafood Chowder

| Cooking time: 6 to 8 hours | Attention: Minimal |

Straight from the slow cooker to the table—serve this classic Seafood Chowder with your favorite soup crackers.

> One 14-ounce (398-g) can **diced tomatoes** with sweet onion, undrained
>
> One 13-ounce (390-ml) can **evaporated milk**
>
> 1/2 teaspoon salt
>
> 1/4 teaspoon freshly ground black pepper
>
> 1 1/2 pounds (683 g) firm **fish fillets**, such as haddock or cod

Put the diced tomatoes, evaporated milk, salt, and pepper in the slow cooker and stir to combine. Add the fish fillets and stir to moisten them. Cover and cook on LOW for 6 to 8 hours, or until the fish can easily be flaked with a fork.

To serve, break the fish fillets into bite-size chunks. Stir the chowder and season it with additional salt and pepper, if desired.

YIELD: 6 servings

ADD IT! Add 4 medium potatoes, peeled and cubed.

NUTRITIONAL ANALYSIS: One serving of the basic recipe (made with haddock fillets) contains 198 calories; 6 g fat; 27 g protein; 10 g carbohydrate; and 1 g dietary fiber.

TRY THIS

This is a perfect dish to pour into thermoses and take to the park or the game on a cold day.

Shrimp and Mushroom Marinara

Cooking time: 2 1/2 to 3 1/2 hours

Attention: Add another ingredient during final 15 to 30 minutes; watch to prevent overcooking

Shrimp and mushrooms in red sauce is a perennial favorite. Serve over angel hair pasta, linguine, or penne pasta, topped with shredded mozzarella or Parmesan cheese. For a change of pace, serve bread and olive oil for dipping as a healthful alternative to garlic bread.

One 26-ounce (735-g) jar **marinara sauce**

1 cup (100 g) **sliced mushrooms**

3/4 teaspoon salt

1/4 teaspoon freshly ground black pepper

1 pound (455 g) **frozen cooked shrimp**, thawed and deveined

Put the marinara sauce, sliced mushrooms, salt, and pepper in the slow cooker and stir to combine. Cover and cook on LOW for 2 to 3 hours, or until the mushrooms are thoroughly cooked and the flavors have melded.

Add the thawed shrimp and stir. Cover and cook for another 15 to 30 minutes, or just until the shrimp are thoroughly warmed; do not overcook or the shrimp will become tough.

YIELD: 5 generous servings

NUTRITIONAL ANALYSIS: One serving of the basic recipe contains 178 calories; 4 g fat; 21 g protein; 13 g carbohydrate; and 3 g dietary fiber.

TRY THIS

For another favorite dish, substitute clams for the shrimp.

Shrimp Creole

Cooking time: 6 1/2 to 8 1/2 hours on LOW   3 1/2 to 4 1/2 hours on HIGH
Attention: Add another ingredient during final 15 to 30 minutes;
            watch to prevent overcooking

This is a traditional Creole favorite made simple using your slow cooker. Enjoy today with dirty rice, fried okra, and cornbread. Tomorrow, enjoy the leftovers, which taste even better.

> One 32-ounce (905-g) jar onion-and-garlic-flavored **pasta sauce**
>
> 1 1/2 cups (340 g) frozen **Seasoning-Blend Vegetables** (page 30), thawed
>
> 3/4 teaspoon salt
>
> 1/4 teaspoon freshly ground black pepper
>
> 1 1/2 pounds (683 g) **frozen cooked shrimp**, thawed, shelled, and deveined

Put the pasta sauce, thawed vegetables, salt, and pepper in the slow cooker and stir to combine. Cook on LOW for 6 to 8 hours or on HIGH for 3 to 4 hours.

Add the thawed shrimp to the sauce mixture and stir again. Cover and cook for another 15 to 30 minutes, or until the shrimp are thoroughly warmed; do not overcook or the shrimp will become tough.

YIELD: 8 generous servings

ADD IT! Add 2 to 6 drops hot sauce along with the shrimp to kick up the heat.

DID YOU KNOW?

Dirty rice is a traditional soul food dish made with chicken livers and gizzards, ground beef, onions, garlic, green onions, peppers, celery, salt and pepper. You can find recipes on Web sites such as www.chitterlings.com and www.zatarain.com.

Sweet-and-Sour Shrimp

Cooking time: 2 1/2 to 3 hours

Attention: Add another ingredient during final 15 to 30 minutes;
watch to prevent overcooking

Who can resist Sweet-and-Sour Shrimp with Asian-blend vegetables over fluffy white rice? Pick your favorite Asian or stir-fry blend of vegetables for this recipe, and enjoy!

One 12-ounce (340-g) bag frozen **Asian-blend vegetables**

3/4 cup (188 g) **sweet-and-sour sauce**

1 pound (455 g) **frozen cooked shrimp**, thawed, shelled, and deveined

Salt and freshly ground black pepper

Put the frozen vegetables and sweet-and-sour sauce in the slow cooker and stir to combine. Cover and cook on LOW for 2 to 2 1/2 hours, or until the vegetables are tender but not mushy.

Add the thawed shrimp to the slow cooker and stir. Cover and cook for another 15 to 30 minutes, or until the shrimp are thoroughly warmed; do not overcook or the shrimp will become tough.

Before serving, stir the mixture and season with salt and pepper to taste.

YIELD: 4 servings

NUTRITIONAL ANALYSIS: One serving of the basic recipe contains 222 calories; 2 g fat; 27 g protein; 25 g carbohydrate; and 4 g dietary fiber.

DID YOU KNOW?
Asian-blend, or stir-fry, vegetables can consist of any combination of these vegetables: broccoli, mushrooms, green beans, onion, water chestnuts, red peppers, sugar snap peas, baby cob corn, carrots, celery, bamboo shoots, edamame.

Szechwan Shrimp

Enjoy this hot-and-spicy shrimp dish over hot white rice.

1/2 cup (120 ml) water

1/4 cup (60 ml) **soy sauce**

2 tablespoons (31 g) **Szechwan hot-and-spicy sauce**

1 pound (455 g) **frozen cooked shrimp**, thawed, shelled, and deveined

Salt and freshly ground black pepper

Put the water, soy sauce, and Szechwan sauce in the slow cooker and stir to combine. Add the thawed shrimp and stir to coat them. Cover and cook on HIGH for 1 to 1 1/2 hours, or until the sauce and shrimp are thoroughly heated.

Before serving, stir the mixture and season with salt and pepper to taste.

YIELD: 4 servings

ADD IT! Substitute chicken broth for the water, and add 2 teaspoons (7 g) minced garlic to the sauce mixture. Thicken the sauce with 1 tablespoon (8 g) cornstarch, and garnish the dish with chopped green onion.

NOTE: The secret to this delicious dish is the rich, spicy flavor of the Szechwan peppercorn in the Szechwan hot-and-spicy sauce.

NUTRITIONAL ANALYSIS: One serving of the basic recipe contains 123 calories; 1 g fat; 25 g protein; 2 g carbohydrate; and .3 g dietary fiber.

TRY THIS

Add a cooling cucumber salad for balance, and then some fortune cookies just for fun!

Shrimp Newburg

For a change of pace, enjoy Shrimp Newburg over toast points or pasta instead of white rice. Sautéed spinach (see "Try This," below) and potato rolls round out this special but simple-to-prepare meal.

10 3/4-ounce (305-g) can **condensed cream of shrimp soup**

2/3 cup (157 ml) **evaporated milk**

1 pound (455 g) **frozen cooked shrimp**, thawed, shelled, and deveined

Salt and freshly ground black pepper

Put the condensed soup and evaporated milk in the slow cooker and stir to combine. Add the thawed shrimp and stir again. Cover and cook on HIGH for 1 to 1 1/2 hours, or until the sauce and shrimp are thoroughly heated.

Before serving, stir the mixture and season with salt and pepper to taste.

YIELD: 4 servings

ADD IT! Add 1 cup (100 g) sliced fresh mushrooms and 1 tablespoon (14 ml) cooking sherry along with the shrimp.

NUTRITIONAL ANALYSIS: One serving of the basic recipe contains 214 calories; 7 g fat; 28 g protein; 8 g carbohydrate; and .3 g dietary fiber.

TRY THIS
It's simple to prepare sautéed spinach. Sauté minced garlic in equal parts butter and olive oil. Add fresh spinach leaves to the skillet, and sauté the spinach just until it's wilted.

Chapter 13

• •

Main Dishes: Vegetarian

Vegetarian fare is fast becoming a centerpiece meal for the mainstream. Many people are starting to promote health by substituting one or more meatless meals a week. A vegetarian diet is associated with major health benefits because of the vitamins, the minerals, and the cancer-fighting phytochemicals and dietary fiber that beans, legumes, and vegetables supply. But you know all that! You're turning to this chapter because vegetarian meals are a natural for the slow cooker—easy to prepare and serve, with a surefire, delicious result. You know just how rich and satisfying dinner can be when the main dish is a steaming bowl of Santa Fe Black Beans and Corn (page 178), Ravioli Stew (page 188), or even Vegetarian Sloppy Joes (page 192) for the kids. Your family won't even know the meat's missing—because it's all about great taste!

No~Frill Beans

Cooking time: 8 to 10 hours on LOW   4 to 5 hours on HIGH
Attention: Minimal

You might want to cook up batches of dried beans in your slow cooker, some to use right away and some to freeze for later. That way, you'll always have a nice assortment of beans in the freezer, ready to pop into a recipe. A scant 1 1/4 cups of cooked beans is approximately equivalent to a 14-ounce (398-g) can of beans.

> 1 pound (455 g) **dried beans**
>
> 1 1/2 quarts (1.4 L) water
>
> 2 **onions**, chopped
>
> 2 to 3 cloves **garlic**, minced

Put the beans in a large colander, pick through them to remove any debris, and rinse them under running water. Put them in a large bowl, cover them with water, and let them soak for 6 to 8 hours, or overnight.

Pour the beans back into the colander, discarding the used water, and rinse the beans again under running water. Place the beans in the slow cooker and add the 1 1/2 quarts (1.4 L) water, chopped onions, and minced garlic. Cover and cook on LOW for 8 to 10 hours or on HIGH for 4 to 5 hours.

Return the beans to the colander, drain them, and rinse them under running water once more. Use them in a recipe, or allow them to cool and then freeze them for later use.

YIELD: 10 servings

NUTRITIONAL ANALYSIS: One serving of the basic recipe contains 161 calories; .6 g fat; 10 g protein; 30 g carbohydrate; and 12 g dietary fiber.

Special Baked Beans

Cooking time: 4 to 6 hours	Attention: Minimal

There are almost as many ways to make baked beans as there are cooks. Bring this special recipe to the picnic or to that important family get-together. Or, make it the centerpiece of a vegetarian meal, served with 7-grain rolls or wheat-berry bread.

One 28-ounce (795-g) can **vegetarian baked beans**

1/2 cup (120 g) vegetarian **ketchup**

1/4 cup (56 g) **brown sugar**, packed

Salt and freshly ground black pepper

Put the canned baked beans, ketchup, and brown sugar in the slow cooker and stir to combine. Cover and cook on LOW for 4 to 6 hours.

Before serving, stir the mixture again and season it with salt and pepper to taste.

YIELD: 6 servings

ADD IT! Add 1 pound (455 g) meatless sausage, ground-style or chopped into small pieces, 1/2 cup (65 g) chopped onion, and 1 teaspoon (3 g) minced garlic, and increase the cooking time to 6 to 9 hours.

NUTRITIONAL ANALYSIS: One serving of the basic recipe contains 178 calories; .7 g fat; 7 g protein; 42 g carbohydrate; and 7 g dietary fiber.

TRY THIS

Don't forget the sides! Beans and rice make a balanced protein meal. Add a crisp green salad packed with colorful chopped veggies for a filling, delicious meal.

Santa Fe Black Beans and Corn

Cooking time: 3 to 4 hours　　　　　　**Attention:** Minimal

Serve this deceptively simple main dish rolled in corn tortillas or spooned over Yellow Rice (page 227). For a change of pace, serve it as a nacho topping or as a dip accompanied by blue tortilla chips for scoops.

　　Two 15-ounce (417-g) cans **Mexican corn** with red and green peppers

　　One 15-ounce (417-g) can **black beans**, rinsed and drained

　　1 cup (225 g) **chunky-style salsa**

Put the Mexican corn, black beans, and salsa in the slow cooker and stir to combine. Cover and cook on LOW for 3 to 4 hours.

YIELD: 6 servings

ADD IT! Sprinkle 1 cup (115 g) shredded Mexican-blend cheese over the mixture 15 minutes before it's done and continue cooking until the cheese has melted.

NUTRITIONAL ANALYSIS: One serving of the basic recipe contains 195 calories; 4 g fat; 8 g protein; 36 g carbohydrate; and 7 g dietary fiber.

TRY THIS

Here's a simple trick: If you want to serve this dish as a dip, give it a creamier texture by mashing it with a potato masher before serving. Stir well, pour into a bowl, and top with more salsa and some sour cream. Pass the chopped green onions and sliced olives!

Black Bean Chili

Cooking time: 8 to 10 hours on LOW   4 to 5 hours on HIGH
Attention: Minimal

Nothing's better on a cold, blustery day than a big steaming bowl of chili. Serve with a slab of cornbread smothered in butter.

> Two 14 1/2-ounce (413-g) cans Mexican-flavored **stewed tomatoes**
>
> One 15-ounce (417-g) can **vegetarian chili**, with or without beans
>
> One 15-ounce (417-g) can ready-to-eat **black bean soup**
>
> Salt and freshly ground black pepper

Put the stewed tomatoes, chili, and black bean soup in the slow cooker and stir to combine. Cover and cook on LOW for 8 to 10 hours or on HIGH for 4 to 5 hours.

Before serving, stir the mixture again and season it with salt and pepper to taste.

YIELD: 6 servings

ADD IT! Add an undrained 17-ounce (483-g) can Mexican-style whole-kernel corn with peppers, 1 1/2 cups (340 g) frozen Seasoning-Blend Vegetables (page 30), a 1.25-ounce (35-g) envelope chili seasoning mix, and 2 cloves garlic, minced.

NUTRITIONAL ANALYSIS: One serving of the basic recipe (made with vegetarian chili without beans) contains 165 calories; 2 g fat; 16 g protein; 25 g carbohydrate; and 5 g dietary fiber.

TRY THIS

Substitute another type of canned bean soup to give your chili a subtly different flavor.

Vegetarian Hoppin' John

Cooking time: 6 to 8 hours on LOW   3 to 5 hours on HIGH
Attention: Minimal

Hoppin' John is served on New Year's Day for good luck in the coming year. Make today your lucky day. Enjoy an overflowing bowl of black-eyed peas and rice, with Collard Greens (page 205) and cornbread on the side.

3/4 cup (175 ml) hot water

1 vegetable **bouillon cube**

One 14-ounce (398-g) can **diced tomatoes** with green chilies, undrained

One 7-ounce (197-g) package **black-eyed peas** and rice mix

Salt and freshly ground black pepper

Put the hot water and bouillon cube in the slow cooker and stir until the bouillon cube has dissolved. Add the diced tomatoes and black-eyed peas and rice mix, and stir again. Cover and cook on LOW for 6 to 8 hours or on HIGH for 3 to 5 hours.

Before serving, stir the mixture and season it with salt and pepper to taste.

YIELD: 8 servings

ADD IT! Add 1 medium onion, chopped, and 3 cloves garlic, minced, along with the diced tomatoes and black-eyed peas and rice mix.

NUTRITIONAL ANALYSIS: One serving of the basic recipe contains 97 calories; .4 g fat; .7 g protein; 18 g carbohydrate; and 7 g dietary fiber.

DID YOU KNOW?

No one is sure how Hoppin' John got its name, but this traditional Southern dish made from black-eyed peas and rice dates to at least the 1800s.

Saucy Italian Chick Peas

Cooking time: 6 to 8 hours on LOW   3 to 4 hours on HIGH
Attention: Minimal

This is a super simple dish to throw together for a light but healthful dinner. Serve it over pasta shells, topped with Parmesan cheese, or eat it all by itself.

Two 14-ounce (398-g) cans **diced tomatoes** with garlic, oregano, and basil, undrained

One 19-ounce (540-g) can **chick peas**, rinsed and drained

1 teaspoon **Italian Seasoning** (page 29)

Salt and freshly ground black pepper

Put the diced tomatoes, chick peas, and Italian Seasoning in the slow cooker and stir to combine. Cover and cook on LOW for 6 to 8 hours or on HIGH for 3 to 4 hours.

Before serving, stir the mixture again and season it with salt and pepper to taste.

YIELD: 6 servings

ADD IT! Add 2 large cloves garlic, minced, and 1/8 teaspoon chili flakes.

NUTRITIONAL ANALYSIS: One serving of the basic recipe contains 140 calories; 1 g fat; 7 g protein; 27 g carbohydrate; and 6 g dietary fiber.

DID YOU KNOW?

Chick peas and garbanzos are two names for the same legume. They're also the base for hummus.

Field Peas with Snaps and Rice

Cooking time: 4 to 5 hours   **Attention:** Minimal

Enjoy this Southern specialty with the traditional accompaniment, cornbread, or with flaky biscuits slathered with Apricot Preserves (page 104).

    2 vegetable **bouillon cubes**

    2 cups (475 ml) hot water

    One 15-ounce (417-g) can **field peas** with snaps

    3/4 cup (139 g) raw **long-grain white rice**

    Salt and freshly ground black pepper

Put the hot water and bouillon cubes in the slow cooker and stir until the bouillon cubes have dissolved. Add the field peas with snaps and dry rice, and stir again. Cover and cook on LOW for 4 to 5 hours, or until the rice is tender.

Before serving, stir the mixture and season it with salt and pepper to taste. This dish tastes especially good with lots of pepper.

YIELD: 6 servings

NUTRITIONAL ANALYSIS: One serving of the basic recipe contains 143 calories; .8 g fat; 5 g protein; 28 g carbohydrate; and 3 g dietary fiber.

DID YOU KNOW?
Field peas with snaps are actually the beans known worldwide as cowpeas. Immature pods—only the youngest and most tender—are typically broken into a batch of field peas, and these are called snaps.

❧ Northern Bean Soup

Cooking time: 8 to 10 hours on LOW   4 to 6 hours on HIGH
Attention: Mash beans during final 1 to 2 hours; add another ingredient during final 30 minutes

This vegetarian soup is healthful and delicious. Enjoy with hot buttered cornbread on cold winter days.

Two 15-ounce (417-g) cans **Great Northern beans** or **navy beans**, rinsed and drained

Two 10³⁄₄-ounce (305-g) cans **condensed vegetarian vegetable soup**

³⁄₄ cup (175 ml) water

3 tablespoons (45 ml) **olive oil**

Salt and freshly ground black pepper

Put the beans, condensed soup, and water in the slow cooker and stir to combine. Cover and cook on LOW for 8 to 10 hours or on HIGH for 4 to 6 hours.

Between 1 and 2 hours before the soup is done, thicken the soup by mashing the beans with a potato masher. About 30 minutes before the soup is done, add the olive oil and mix well. Just before serving, stir the soup again and season it with salt and pepper to taste.

YIELD: 6 servings

ADD IT! Add 10 ounces (280 g) meatless sausage cut into bite-size pieces and 2 teaspoons (10 ml) vegetarian Worcestershire sauce along with the beans and condensed soup.

NUTRITIONAL ANALYSIS: One serving of the basic recipe (made with Great Northern beans) contains 270 calories; 9 g fat; 12 g protein; 38 g carbohydrate; and 7 g dietary fiber.

TRY THIS

Make a rich variation on this soup by adding sautéed onions and mushrooms. Add sliced black olives in the final half-hour of cooking.

Garlic~Barbecue Baked Beans

Cooking time: 8 to 10 hours   **Attention:** Minimal

Baked beans are a staple of the vegetarian diet. Enjoy this garlicky version with a tossed salad and crusty bread.

 Two 15-ounce (417-g) cans **Great Northern beans**, rinsed and drained

 1 1/2 cups (375 g) garlic-flavored **barbecue sauce**

 1 **onion**, chopped

 Salt and freshly ground black pepper

Put the Great Northern beans, barbecue sauce, and chopped onion in the slow cooker and stir to combine. Cover and cook on LOW for 8 to 10 hours.

Before serving, stir the mixture again and season it with salt and pepper to taste.

YIELD: 6 servings

NUTRITIONAL ANALYSIS: One serving of the basic recipe contains 216 calories; 2 g fat; 12 g protein; 39 g carbohydrate; and 8 g dietary fiber.

TRY THIS

Non-vegetarians, take note: These spicy barbecued beans are great at picnics and wiener roasts.

Bean, Barley, and Mock-Sausage Stew

Cooking time: 8 to 10 hours	**Attention:** Minimal

Don't you love the smell of slow-cooking stew on a cold winter's day? Serve this aromatic and full-flavored stew with Maple-Glazed Baby Carrots (page 203) and sourdough bread.

Two 15-ounce (417-g) cans light **red kidney beans**, rinsed and drained

3 1/2 cups (823 ml) water

1 pound (455 g) **meatless Italian sausage**, cut into chunks

1 cup (200 g) uncooked **pearl barley**

Salt

Put the kidney beans, water, mock sausage, and pearl barley in the slow cooker and stir to combine. Cover and cook on LOW for 8 to 10 hours.

Before serving, stir the stew again and season it with salt to taste.

YIELD: 8 servings

ADD IT! Substitute vegetable broth for the water, and add 1/2 cup (65 g) chopped onion and 2 cloves garlic, minced.

NUTRITIONAL ANALYSIS: One serving of the basic recipe contains 324 calories; 11 g fat; 19 g protein; 42 g carbohydrate; and 12 g dietary fiber.

TRY THIS

Not a fan of mock meats? Substitute one of the many flavored tofus now on the market. They're available at most grocery stores.

🌾 Barley Casserole

The mildly nutty flavor of barley combines superbly with mixed vegetables in a tomato-based broth. Serve with cornbread or hush puppies for a delicious meal.

Two 19-ounce (540-g) cans ready-to-eat vegetarian **vegetable soup**

1 cup (200 g) uncooked **pearl barley**

1 tablespoon (14 ml) **Worcestershire sauce**

Salt and freshly ground black pepper

Put the vegetable soup, pearl barley, and Worcestershire sauce in the slow cooker and stir to combine. Cover and cook on LOW for 6 to 10 hours, or until the barley is tender.

Before serving, stir the casserole again and season it with salt and pepper to taste.

YIELD: 6 servings

ADD IT! Add a drained 15-ounce (417-g) can garbanzo beans and 2 to 10 drops hot sauce.

NUTRITIONAL ANALYSIS: One serving of the basic recipe contains 173 calories; 2 g fat; 5 g protein; 35 g carbohydrate; and 6 g dietary fiber.

TRY THIS

If you like thick hot breakfast grains like oatmeal or cream of wheat, you should try this barley dish for breakfast. It will start your day off right!

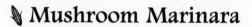 Mushroom Marinara

Cooking time: 6 to 7 hours   **Attention:** Minimal

This tasty, versatile sauce also goes great over cooked pasta, meat, or chicken. For a distinctive vegetarian treat, serve over spinach-and-cheese-stuffed manicotti, served with rustic Italian bread.

One 32-ounce (905-g) jar **marinara sauce**

1 1/2 cups (340 g) frozen **Seasoning-Blend Vegetables** (page 30), thawed

One 12-ounce (340-g) bag frozen **sliced mushrooms**, thawed

Salt and freshly ground black pepper

Put the marinara sauce, thawed vegetables, and thawed mushrooms in the slow cooker and stir to combine. Cover and cook on LOW for 6 to 7 hours.

Before serving, stir the mixture again and season it with salt and pepper to taste.

YIELD: 8 servings

NUTRITIONAL ANALYSIS: One serving of the basic recipe contains 97 calories; 3 g fat; 4 g protein; 16 g carbohydrate; and 4 g dietary fiber.

IT'S GOOD FOR YOU
Trade mushrooms for meat? Not such a novel idea. The vitamin content of mushrooms resembles that of meat, yet mushrooms are very low in calories, are fat-free, and contain fiber. What a deal!

◣ Ravioli Stew

Cooking time: 45 to 60 minutes

Attention: Add another ingredient after 30 minutes

"Quick and easy" best describes this ravioli dish. But the taste—now, that's indescribable. Ladle into shallow bowls, top with your favorite grated cheese, and enjoy with garlic breadsticks fresh from the oven.

> One 32-ounce (905-g) jar chunky garden-style **pasta sauce**
>
> 2 teaspoons (1.6 g) dried **basil**
>
> One 9-ounce (255-g) package refrigerated **cheese ravioli**

Put the pasta sauce and dried basil in the slow cooker and stir to combine. Cover and cook on HIGH for 30 minutes, or until the sauce is hot and bubbly.

Add the ravioli and stir. Cover and cook for another 15 to 30 minutes, or until the ravioli are tender but not mushy.

YIELD: 4 servings

ADD IT! Add a 15-ounce (417-g) can cannelloni beans, rinsed and drained, to the pasta sauce, and cook the mixture on HIGH for 1 hour instead of 30 minutes. Add $1/8$ teaspoon crushed red pepper along with the ravioli, and cook for another 15 to 30 minutes.

NUTRITIONAL ANALYSIS: One serving of the basic recipe contains 116 calories; 5 g fat; 6 g protein; 13 g carbohydrate; and .8 g dietary fiber.

TRY THIS

You can substitute tortellini or gnocchi for the ravioli.

❧ Three-Cheese Vegetarian Spaghetti

Cooking time: 6 to 8 hours on LOW   3 to 4 hours on HIGH

Attention: Change heat setting and add another ingredient during final hour

Preparing a delicious, home-cooked spaghetti dinner for your family is a labor of love—or it used to be. This delicious one-pot spaghetti dish gives you some labor-free time away from the kitchen.

> One 28-ounce (795-g) jar three-cheese-flavored **pasta sauce**
>
> 12 ounces (340 g) **imitation ground burger**
>
> 6 ounces (168 g) **dry spaghetti**, broken into 4-inch (10-cm) pieces

Put the pasta sauce and imitation ground burger in the slow cooker and stir to combine. Cover and cook on LOW for 6 to 8 hours or on HIGH for 3 to 4 hours.

An hour before the dish is done, add the dry spaghetti and stir. Cook on HIGH for 1 more hour, or until the spaghetti is tender but not mushy.

YIELD: 4 servings

NUTRITIONAL ANALYSIS: One serving of the basic recipe contains 411 calories; 1 g fat; 61 g protein; 49 g carbohydrate; and 17 g dietary fiber.

TRY THIS

Substitute sliced mushrooms for the imitation ground burger. You can also vary the flavor of the spaghetti by using black bean burgers or other flavors. Substitute macaroni for the spaghetti to give this dish a new twist.

Mock Meaty Pasta Sauce

Cooking time: 6 to 8 hours on LOW   3 to 4 hours on HIGH
Attention: Minimal

The supermarket shelves are crowded with good pasta sauces. Grab your favorite, and with a little help from your slow cooker, you can get a wonderful, full-bodied, meaty sauce. You'll know it's vegetarian, but will anyone else?

One 28-ounce (795-g) jar vegetarian **pasta sauce**

12 ounces (340 g) **imitation ground burger**

1 1/2 cups (340 g) frozen **Seasoning-Blend Vegetables** (page 30)

Salt and freshly ground black pepper

Put the pasta sauce, imitation ground burger, and frozen vegetables in the slow cooker and stir to combine. Cover and cook on LOW for 6 to 8 hours or on HIGH for 3 to 4 hours.

Just before serving, stir the sauce again and season it with salt and pepper to taste.

YIELD: 10 servings

ADD IT! Add 2 cloves garlic, minced.

NUTRITIONAL ANALYSIS: One serving of the basic recipe contains 119 calories; 4 g fat; 23 g protein; 11 g carbohydrate; and 7.3 g dietary fiber.

TRY THIS

Deepen the flavor of your sauce with one or more of these "secret ingredients:" a half-cup of red wine (like Chianti), a teaspoon of sugar, or a tablespoon of chutney. Add them in the last half-hour of cooking for a richer-tasting sauce.

❦ Cheesy Italian Casserole

Cooking time: 6 ½ to 7 ½ hours
Attention: Add another ingredient during final 10 to 15 minutes

This easy meal is made irresistible by the yummy goodness of mozzarella cheese. Serve over pasta, with grated Parmesan and garlic toast.

One 32-ounce (905-g) jar chunky-style **pasta sauce** with mushrooms

12 ounces (340 g) **imitation ground burger**

¼ teaspoon freshly ground black pepper

1 cup (112 g) shredded **Italian** or **mozzarella cheese**

Put the pasta sauce, imitation ground burger, and pepper in the slow cooker and stir to combine. Cover and cook on LOW for 6 to 7 hours.

Stir the casserole again and sprinkle it with the cheese. Cover and cook for another 10 to 15 minutes, or until the cheese has melted.

YIELD: 8 servings

ADD IT! About 30 minutes before the casserole is done, stir in 2 cups total of any or all of these veggies, all lightly steamed: broccoli, cauliflower, zucchini, carrots.

NUTRITIONAL ANALYSIS: One serving of the basic recipe (made with shredded mozzarella cheese) contains 172 calories; 4 g fat; 31 g protein; 9 g carbohydrate; and 8 g dietary fiber.

TRY THIS

If you have leftover sauce, try it Sloppy-Joe style over a whole-wheat bun.

❧ Vegetarian Sloppy Joes

Cooking time: 5 to 9 hours on LOW   2 1/2 to 4 hours on HIGH
Attention: Minimal

Kids—from 3 to 103—love Sloppy Joes.

> 12 ounces (340 g) **imitation ground burger**, browned and drained
>
> One 15-ounce (417-g) can **vegetarian chili** with beans
>
> 1/2 cup (125 g) **barbecue sauce**
>
> Salt and freshly ground black pepper

In a large skillet over medium heat, brown the imitation ground burger. Drain it well, then place it in the slow cooker.

Add the chili and barbecue sauce to the browned imitation meat and stir to combine. Cover and cook on LOW for 5 to 9 hours or on HIGH for 2 1/2 to 3 hours.

Stir the mixture again and season it with salt and pepper to taste. Serve it on hamburger buns.

YIELD: 8 servings

ADD IT! Add 1 cup (227 g) frozen Seasoning-Blend Vegetables (page 30), 2 teaspoons (10 ml) Worcestershire sauce, and 2 cloves garlic, minced.

NUTRITIONAL ANALYSIS: One serving of the basic recipe contains 208 calories; 2 g fat; 37 g protein; 18 g carbohydrate; and 10 g dietary fiber.

TRY THIS

Spice up your Sloppy Joes with chopped onion and/or ground cumin. Serve them with sweet potato fries and coleslaw for a scrumptious meal!

❧ Chili Hot Dogs

Cooking time: 4 to 5 hours on LOW   2 to 2 1/2 hours on HIGH
Attention: Minimal

Hot dog fanatics will love being able to dip into the slow cooker for the makings for a chili dog. Serve on toasted rolls, and top with cheddar cheese and green onion.

    8 **vegetarian hot dogs**

    One 15-ounce (417-g) can **vegetarian chili** with beans

    1 large **onion**, chopped

    Salt and freshly ground black pepper

Put the hot dogs, chili, and chopped onion in the slow cooker and stir to combine. Cover and cook on LOW for 4 to 5 hours or on HIGH for 2 to 2 1/2 hours.

Just before serving, stir the mixture again and season it with salt and pepper to taste.

YIELD: 8 servings

ADD IT! Add 1 teaspoon chili powder.

NUTRITIONAL ANALYSIS: One serving of the basic recipe contains 194 calories; 8 g fat; 22 g protein; 10 g carbohydrate; and 4 g dietary fiber.

TRY THIS

This recipe works well with vegetarian meatballs, or, for that matter, real meatballs!

Chapter 14

• •

Vegetables and Other Side Dishes

Side dishes are designed to round out the nutrition of a meal, as well as to set off the entrée by adding interest, variety, and color. Many slow-cooker side dishes, such as our White Beans with Sun-Dried Tomatoes (page 210), are hearty enough to function as a main dish as well. Some side dishes go exceptionally well with certain main dishes; a good example is Candied Sweet Potatoes (page 223), which is great with any holiday meal. Others—say, Fabulous Foil Potatoes (page 213)—can be paired with just about any main dish. So, when you want to try a little color next to your main course, check out our Cheesy California Vegetables (page 197), Rustic Mashed Potatoes (page 219), or Maple-Apple Sweet Potatoes (page 222). And when you just want to make it easier to get everything on the table at the same time, pick any slow-cooker side dish you wish!

☛ Easiest Vegetable~Surprise Dish

Cooking time: 1 1/2 to 2 1/2 hours on LOW   45 to 75 minutes on HIGH
Attention: Minimal

The surprise is that this dish is so quick and easy. While you run to the gym, you can be cooking a healthful veggie side dish.

Two 16-ounce (455-g) bags **frozen mixed vegetables**, partially thawed

One 10 3/4-ounce (305-g) can **condensed cream of mushroom or cream of celery soup**

1 small **onion**, chopped

1/2 teaspoon salt

Put the partially thawed vegetables, condensed soup, chopped onion, and salt in the slow cooker and stir to combine. Cover and cook on LOW for 1 1/2 to 2 1/2 hours or on HIGH for 45 to 75 minutes.

YIELD: 8 servings

NUTRITIONAL ANALYSIS: One serving of the basic recipe (made with condensed cream of mushroom soup) contains 117 calories; 4 g fat; 5 g protein; 19 g carbohydrate; and 5 g dietary fiber.

IT'S GOOD FOR YOU

Did you know that frozen veggies are better for you than fresh ones? This isn't true if you shop for organic produce. But if you buy conventionally grown vegetables, they're sprayed with insecticides and fungicides to ensure a flawless appearance. Since appearance isn't an issue with frozen veggies, they're not sprayed as often and have less chemical residue than their fresh counterparts.

☙ Cheesy California Vegetables

Cooking time: 1 1/2 to 2 1/2 hours on LOW   45 to 75 minutes on HIGH
Attention: Minimal

You'll enjoy the cheesy taste of these sweet California vegetables even more because fixing them was so quick and easy. Broccoli, cauliflower, carrots—you never had them so good.

Two 16-ounce (455-g) bags frozen **California-blend vegetables**, partially thawed

One 10 3/4-ounce (305-g) can **condensed cheddar cheese soup**

2 cloves **garlic**, minced

1/2 teaspoon salt

Put the partially thawed vegetables, condensed soup, minced garlic, and salt in the slow cooker and stir to combine. Cover and cook on LOW for 1 1/2 to 2 1/2 hours or on HIGH for 45 to 75 minutes.

YIELD: 8 servings

NUTRITIONAL ANALYSIS: One serving of the basic recipe contains 113 calories; 3 g fat; 5 g protein; 18 g carbohydrate; and 5 g dietary fiber.

TRY THIS

Substitute mixed corn and lima beans for the California vegetables for another great side dish.

▼ Creamy Veggie Casserole

Cooking time: 8 to 10 hours on LOW   4 to 5 hours on HIGH
Attention: Minimal

Super simple and super delicious. Enjoy this side dish with virtually any meal.

2 1/2 cups (588 ml) hot water

3 chicken **bouillon cubes**

6 cups (720 g) frozen **stew vegetables**, partially thawed

Two 10 3/4-ounce (305-g) cans **condensed cream of chicken soup**

Put the hot water and bouillon cubes in the slow cooker and stir until the bouillon cubes have dissolved. Add the partially thawed vegetables and condensed soup, and stir again. Cover and cook on LOW for 8 to 10 hours or on HIGH for 4 to 5 hours, or until the vegetables are tender.

YIELD: 12 servings

ADD IT! For a richer taste, add 5 1/2 tablespoons (1/3 cup, or 75 g) butter, melted, and 2 tablespoons (8 g) chopped fresh parsley.

NUTRITIONAL ANALYSIS: One serving of the basic recipe contains 100 calories; 3 g fat; 4 g protein; 16 g carbohydrate; and 4 g dietary fiber.

TRY THIS

If you have leftover cooked chicken, add it to this recipe, then serve over rice or cornbread for a satisfying main dish.

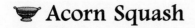 Acorn Squash

Cooking time: 8 to 10 hours   **Attention:** Minimal

This is just too simple! Pair Acorn Squash with Chunky Applesauce (page 242) and your favorite entrée.

1 1/2- to 2-pound (683- to 910-g) whole **acorn squash**, rinsed well

2 teaspoons (12 g) salt

1/2 teaspoon freshly ground black pepper

6 tablespoons (84 g) **butter**, melted

2 tablespoons (28 g) **brown sugar**, packed

Pierce the acorn squash in several places with a fork and place it in the slow cooker. Cover and cook on LOW for 8 to 10 hours, or until the squash is fork-tender.

Remove the squash from the slow cooker and allow it to cool enough to be handled safely. Cut the squash in half, then cut each half in half. Scoop out and discard the seeds, place each squash quarter pulp side up on a plate, and season each squash quarter with one-fourth of the salt and pepper. In a small bowl, combine the melted butter and brown sugar, then pour one-fourth of the mixture over each squash quarter.

YIELD: 4 servings

TIP: Place the cooked, seasoned squash quarters on a baking sheet, then fill them with the butter–brown sugar mixture. Warm the squash quarters in a 350°F (180°C) oven for 10 minutes, or until the brown sugar has melted.

NUTRITIONAL ANALYSIS: One serving of the basic recipe (made with a 1 1/2-pound acorn squash) contains 231 calories; 18 g fat; 1 g protein; 20 g carbohydrate; and 2 g dietary fiber.

IT'S GOOD FOR YOU

Acorn squash is an excellent source of vitamin C, vitamin A, magnesium, and potassium. It's also a good source of calcium.

🍲 Asparagus Side Dish

Cooking time: 4 to 6 hours   **Attention:** Minimal

A delicious side dish without comparison. Serve this tempting fare with any Italian entrée for a real treat.

> 1 1/2 pounds (683 g) **asparagus**, sliced diagonally into 1-inch (2.5-cm) pieces
>
> One 10 3/4-ounce (305-g) can **condensed cream of celery soup**
>
> 3/4 cup (86 g) coarsely crushed **saltine crackers**

Spray the inside of the slow cooker with cooking spray.

Place the asparagus pieces in the slow cooker, pour the condensed soup over them, and sprinkle them with the cracker crumbs. Cover and cook on LOW for 4 to 6 hours.

YIELD: 6 servings

ADD IT! Add 1 cup (120 g) grated cheddar when the asparagus has finished cooking. Cover and heat on LOW for another 15 to 30 minutes, or until the cheese has melted. Stir the mixture before serving it.

NUTRITIONAL ANALYSIS: One serving of the basic recipe contains 89 calories; 3 g fat; 3 g protein; 13 g carbohydrate; and 2 g dietary fiber.

TRY THIS

Substitute cream of asparagus soup for the cream of celery soup for an intensely yummy asparagus experience, or add a rich flavor with cream of mushroom soup.

Candied Carrots and Pecans

Cooking time: 6 to 8 hours on LOW   3 to 4 hours on HIGH
Attention: Minimal

Flavored syrup gives this carrot dish a nutty taste. Delicious with pork and wild rice.

    Two 16-ounce (455-g) packages frozen **sliced carrots**

    $3/4$ cup (242 g) **butter pecan-flavored syrup**

    $1/2$ cup (113 g) **brown sugar**, packed

Put the sliced carrots, syrup, and brown sugar in the slow cooker and stir to combine. Cover and cook on LOW for 6 to 8 hours or on HIGH for 3 to 4 hours.

YIELD: 8 servings

ADD IT! Add 1 cup (109 g) chopped pecans, and cook the dish on HIGH for 5 $1/2$ to 6 $1/2$ hours. Do not cook this dish on LOW if you add the nuts.

NUTRITIONAL ANALYSIS: One serving of the basic recipe contains 95 calories; .1 g fat; 1 g protein; 24 g carbohydrate; and 3 g dietary fiber.

> **TRY THIS**
>
> Substitute maple syrup for the butter-pecan syrup, or try this dish with precooked mashed sweet potatoes.

Glazed Crinkle Carrots

Cooking time: 4 to 6 hours on LOW   2 to 3 hours on HIGH
Attention: Stir every hour

For a change of pace, cash in on the fabulous sweet-and-sour taste of these glazed carrot coins.

    8 large **carrots**, sliced into crinkle-cut coins

    ½ cup (113 g) **brown sugar**, packed

    ¼ cup (60 g) **Dijon mustard**

Put the crinkle-cut carrots, brown sugar, and mustard in the slow cooker and stir to combine. Cover and cook on LOW for 4 to 6 hours or on HIGH for 2 to 3 hours, or until the carrot slices are tender, stirring once an hour.

YIELD: 8 servings

ADD IT! Add 1 teaspoon minced fresh ginger.

NUTRITIONAL ANALYSIS: One serving of the basic recipe contains 88 calories; .5 g fat; 1 g protein; 21 g carbohydrate; and 2 g dietary fiber.

TRY THIS

Replace the brown sugar with honey for a different flavor. You can also experiment with the many flavored mustards on the market to find your family's favorite.

🏺 Maple-Glazed Baby Carrots

Cooking time: 6 to 8 hours on LOW   3 to 4 hours on HIGH
Attention: Stir every hour

Maple flavoring gives these babies a sweet, delicate flavor, making them a perfect accompaniment to chicken, pork, or beef.

2 pounds (910 g) **baby carrots**

1/4 cup (81 g) pure **maple syrup**

2 tablespoons (28 g) **butter**

1/4 teaspoon salt

1/8 teaspoon freshly ground black pepper

Put the baby carrots, maple syrup, butter, salt, and pepper in the slow cooker and stir to combine. Cover and cook on LOW for 6 to 8 hours or on HIGH for 3 to 4 hours, or until the carrots are tender and glazed, stirring once an hour.

YIELD: 10 servings

NUTRITIONAL ANALYSIS: One serving of the basic recipe contains 76 calories; 3 g fat; .8 g protein; 13 g carbohydrate; and 2 g dietary fiber.

IT'S GOOD FOR YOU

Carrots are a superb source of antioxidants including beta-carotene (vitamin A) as well as vitamin C, the B vitamins, potassium, and calcium pectate, which has been shown to lower cholesterol.

Marmalade-Glazed Carrots

Cooking time: 2 1/2 to 4 1/2 hours
Attention: Drain juices and add more ingredients during final 20 to 30 minutes

This medley of tangy-sweet orange marmalade and inherently sweet carrots is divine. You can almost eat this one for dessert.

- 4 cups (488 g) diagonally **sliced carrots**
- 2 1/2 cups (588 ml) water
- 1/2 teaspoon salt
- 4 tablespoons (55 g) **butter or margarine**
- 1/2 cup (75 g) **orange marmalade**

Put the sliced carrots, water, and salt in the slow cooker and stir to combine. Cover and cook on HIGH for 2 to 4 hours, or until the carrot slices are tender.

Turn the heat OFF and allow the slow cooker to cool enough so that you can handle the ceramic pot safely. Drain the carrots well, add the butter and orange marmalade, and stir the mixture. Cover and cook on HIGH for 20 to 30 minutes.

YIELD: 8 servings

ADD IT! Add 1/2 cup (30 g) chopped walnuts along with the butter and marmalade.

NUTRITIONAL ANALYSIS: One serving of the basic recipe (made with butter) contains 102 calories; 6 g fat; .8 g protein; 13 g carbohydrate; and 2 g dietary fiber.

TRY THIS

Try this dish with lime or lemon marmalade instead of orange marmalade, or substitute currant jelly or apricot preserves.

 Collard Greens

Cooking time: 8 to 10 hours   **Attention:** Minimal

Enjoy this Southern favorite with a cabbage-like flavor that pairs so well with ham. Simple, yet hearty and delicious.

- 4 ounces (115 g) **seasoned ham**, sliced
- 2 to 3 pounds (.9 to 1.4 kg) **collard greens**, washed, dried, and stems removed
- 2 cups (475 ml) water
- 1/8 cup (28 ml) **white vinegar**

Put the sliced seasoned ham in the bottom of the slow cooker and place the collard greens on top of it. In a small bowl, combine the water and white vinegar, then pour the mixture over the collard greens. Cover and cook on LOW for 8 to 10 hours.

YIELD: 8 servings

ADD IT! Add 6 red potatoes, quartered, and 1 onion, sliced, along with the collard greens.

NUTRITIONAL ANALYSIS: One serving of the basic recipe (made with 2 pounds collard greens) contains 60 calories; 2 g fat; 5 g protein; 7 g carbohydrate; and 4 g dietary fiber.

IT'S GOOD FOR YOU

Collards are an excellent source of vitamin A, vitamin C, manganese, and folate, and are also a good source of calcium and fiber.

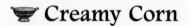 # Creamy Corn

Corn-on-the-cob goodness plus cheese in your slow cooker—without the cob. Enjoy!

> One 16-ounce (455-g) bag **frozen corn**, partially thawed
>
> One 3-ounce (85-g) package **cream cheese**, softened
>
> 2 tablespoons (28 g) **butter**
>
> 1/2 teaspoon salt

Spray the inside of the slow cooker with cooking spray.

Put the partially thawed corn, softened cream cheese, butter, and salt in the slow cooker and stir to combine. Cook on LOW for 1 1/2 to 3 1/2 hours, or until the corn is thoroughly heated and the cream cheese has melted.

YIELD: 4 servings

NUTRITIONAL ANALYSIS: One serving of the basic recipe contains 200 calories; 12 g fat; 5 g protein; 24 g carbohydrate; and 3 g dietary fiber.

TRY THIS

Mmm, mmm, good! Try this dish with sliced frozen carrots or frozen lima beans instead of the corn.

Southern Slow~Cooked Green Beans

Cooking time: 3 1/2 to 4 1/2 hours   **Attention:** Minimal

A simple recipe for fresh green beans that you'll enjoy again and again. Serve in a big bowl with the cooking juices and accompanied by a side of cornbread to sop up the "pot liquor."

1 cup (235 ml) hot water

2 vegetable or chicken **bouillon cubes**

1 quart (440 g) **green beans**, tips removed and beans snapped in half

1 large **onion**, chopped

Salt and freshly ground black pepper

Put the hot water and bouillon cubes in the slow cooker and stir until the bouillon cubes have dissolved. Add the snapped green beans and chopped onion, and stir again. Cover and cook on HIGH for 30 minutes, or until the mixture begins to simmer. Reduce the heat to LOW and simmer the green beans for another 3 to 4 hours.

Stir the green beans and season them with salt and pepper to taste. Serve them in their cooking juices.

YIELD: 6 servings

NUTRITIONAL ANALYSIS: One serving of the basic recipe (made with vegetable bouillon cubes) contains 33 calories; .3 g fat; 2 g protein; 7 g carbohydrate; and 3 g dietary fiber.

TRY THIS

For authentic Southern flavor, add 2 tablespoons of bacon grease to the pot.

☕ Mushrooms Italian

Cooking time: 3 to 4 hours on LOW   1 1/2 to 2 hours on HIGH
Attention: Minimal

Are you mad about mushrooms? This dish has a wonderful Italian essence that doesn't overpower the rich portobello flavor.

>   3 pounds (1.4 kg) whole baby **portobello mushrooms**
>
>   One 10 3/4-ounce (305-g) can **condensed cream of mushroom soup**
>
>   1/2 teaspoon **Italian Seasoning** (page 29)

Put the baby portobello mushrooms, condensed soup, and Italian Seasoning in the slow cooker and mix well. Cover and cook on LOW for 3 to 4 hours or on HIGH for 1 1/2 to 2 hours.

YIELD: 10 servings

ADD IT! Add 1 large sweet onion, very thinly sliced, and 1/4 teaspoon crushed red pepper.

NUTRITIONAL ANALYSIS: One serving of the basic recipe contains 65 calories; 3 g fat; 3 g protein; 8 g carbohydrate; and 2 g dietary fiber.

TRY THIS

Serve these mushrooms over toast or rice with a crisp green salad and sliced tomatoes. The perfect lunch!

🍲 Ranch Mushrooms

Cooking time: 3 to 4 hours on LOW   1 ½ to 2 hours on HIGH
Attention: Minimal

At first glance, mushrooms and ranch dressing seem like an unlikely pairing. But the finished dish reveals the combo to be wonderful!

    2 pounds (910 g) whole **button mushrooms**

    ½ cup (120 ml) garlic-flavored **olive oil**

    Two 1-ounce (28-g) envelopes **ranch salad dressing mix**

Put the button mushrooms, olive oil, and dressing mix in the slow cooker and stir well. Cover and cook on LOW for 3 to 4 hours or on HIGH for 1 ½ to 2 hours.

YIELD: 6 servings

NUTRITIONAL ANALYSIS: One serving of the basic recipe contains 222 calories; 19 g fat; 3 g protein; 12 g carbohydrate; and 2 g dietary fiber.

TRY THIS

Toss these mushrooms with cooked pasta for a delicious side dish or a quick lunch.

☕ White Beans with Sun~Dried Tomatoes

Cooking time: 2 1/2 to 4 1/2 hours on LOW   1 1/2 to 2 1/2 hours on HIGH
Attention: Mash beans and add another ingredient during final 10 minutes

This rich, satisfying dish is redolent with pungent garlic, sweet vine-ripened tomatoes, and lightly herbed olive oil. Enjoy with a Caesar salad and focaccia bread.

Two 15-ounce (417-g) cans lightly seasoned **white beans**, undrained

1/2 cup (60 ml) water

2 to 4 cloves **garlic**, minced

3 ounces (85 g) **Bella Sun Luci Sun Dried Tomatoes** in Olive Oil and Spices, undrained, tomatoes chopped

Salt and freshly ground black pepper

Put the undrained white beans, water, and minced garlic in the slow cooker and stir to combine. Cover and cook on LOW for 2 to 4 hours or on HIGH for 1 to 2 hours.

Mash some of the beans using a potato masher to thicken the mixture. Add the chopped tomatoes with seasoned olive oil, and cook for another 10 minutes, or until the mixture is thoroughly warmed.

Before serving, season the mixture with salt and pepper to taste.

YIELD: 5 servings

NUTRITIONAL ANALYSIS: One serving of the basic recipe contains 24 calories; 3 g fat; 13 g protein; 42 g carbohydrate; and 9 g dietary fiber.

TRY THIS

Substitute vegetable bouillon for the water, and add 1 tablespoon (2.5 g) chopped fresh basil.

☕ Baked Potatoes

Cooking time: 6 to 8 hours on LOW   3 to 4 hours on HIGH
Attention: Minimal

If you had known that baking potatoes in your slow cooker was so easy, wouldn't you have tried it before?

> 6 **baking potatoes**, unpeeled, scrubbed
>
> **Olive oil**
>
> Salt

Rub each potato with olive oil and sprinkle it with salt. Wrap each potato in aluminum foil and place all the potatoes in the slow cooker. Cover and cook on LOW for 6 to 8 hours or on HIGH for 3 to 4 hours, or until the potatoes are fork-tender.

YIELD: 6 servings

NUTRITIONAL ANALYSIS: One serving of the basic recipe (made with 1 tablespoon olive oil per potato) contains 265 calories; 14 g fat; 4 g protein; 33 g carbohydrate; and 3 g dietary fiber.

DID YOU KNOW?

You can cook as few or as many potatoes as you wish in the slow cooker. Just make sure the potatoes fit in one layer on the bottom of the slow cooker, and adjust the cooking time accordingly.

🏺 Pizza Potatoes

Cooking time: 8 to 10 hours on LOW   4 to 5 hours on HIGH
Attention: Minimal

Here are two favorite flavors slow-cooked to perfection. Serve to your favorite teenager for rave reviews.

- 8 medium **potatoes**, peeled and cut in half lengthwise
- 1 ½ cups (340 g) frozen **Seasoning-Blend Vegetables** (page 30), partially thawed
- 2 cups (500 g) **pizza sauce**
- Salt and freshly ground black pepper

Put the potato halves in the slow cooker, cover them with the partially thawed vegetables, and pour the pizza sauce over the vegetables. Cover and cook on LOW for 8 to 10 hours or on HIGH for 4 to 5 hours, or until the potatoes are tender.

Before serving, season the mixture with salt and pepper to taste.

YIELD: 8 servings

ADD IT! Add 8 ounces (225 g) sliced pepperoni to the pizza sauce.

NUTRITIONAL ANALYSIS: One serving of the basic recipe contains 161 calories; 2 g fat; 5 g protein; 33 g carbohydrate; and 3 g dietary fiber.

TRY THIS

Top each serving of Pizza Potatoes with shredded mozzarella and serve with a crisp green salad packed with lots of veggies.

☕ Fabulous Foil Potatoes

Cooking time: 10 to 12 hours　　　　　　　　　**Attention:** Minimal

You may have made these in the oven before. But once you discover that the slow cooker works just as well and requires less attention, that may change. Experiment with seasonings and garnishes for variety.

> 4 medium **potatoes**, unpeeled, scrubbed, and thinly sliced
>
> 2 medium **onions**, very thinly sliced and separated into rings
>
> Salt and freshly ground black pepper
>
> 12 tablespoons (1 1/2 sticks, or 168 g) **butter**

Spray the inside of the slow cooker with cooking spray. Line the slow cooker with enough aluminum foil to enclose all the ingredients.

Put half of the potato slices in the slow cooker and spread them out evenly. Top the potato slices with half of the onion rings. Sprinkle the mixture with salt and pepper and dot it with half of the butter. Layer on the remaining potato slices and onion rings, season the mixture with more salt and pepper, and dot it with the rest of the butter. Crimp the edges of the aluminum foil to seal the contents. Cover and cook on LOW for 10 to 12 hours.

YIELD: 4 servings

NUTRITIONAL ANALYSIS: One serving of the basic recipe contains 422 calories; 35 g fat; 4 g protein; 27 g carbohydrate; and 3 g dietary fiber.

TRY THIS

For a restaurant-quality dish, experiment with a mandoline, a tool for cutting potatoes, cucumbers, carrots, and other produce into uniform, precise slices. Or, for the campfire look, just use a knife and your good judgment.

Saucy Cream-Cheese Potatoes

Cooking time: 6 to 8 hours on LOW   3 to 4 hours on HIGH
Attention: Minimal

Creamy, tender potatoes with just a hint of garlic. Perfect as a side dish or as a lunchtime meal, especially with a scallion garnish.

  6 large **potatoes**, unpeeled, scrubbed, and thinly sliced

  One 8-ounce (225-g) package **cream cheese**, cut into cubes

  1 teaspoon (6 g) **garlic salt**

  1/2 teaspoon freshly ground black pepper

Spray the inside of the slow cooker with cooking spray.

Put one-third of the potato slices in the slow cooker and spread them out evenly. Top them with half of the cream cheese and sprinkle them with half of the garlic salt and pepper. Layer on another third of the potato slices and the rest of the cream cheese, and sprinkle the mixture with the remainder of the garlic salt and pepper. Spread the rest of the potato slices over the top. Cover and cook on LOW for 6 to 8 hours or on HIGH for 3 to 4 hours, or until the potato slices are tender.

Before serving, stir the mixture well.

YIELD: 6 servings

NUTRITIONAL ANALYSIS: One serving of the basic recipe contains 230 calories; 13 g fat; 5 g protein; 23 g carbohydrate; and 2 g dietary fiber.

TRY THIS

For extra color, flavor, and protein, top this dish with shredded Swiss or white cheddar cheese and a sprinkling of paprika just before serving; serve bubbly hot as soon as the cheese melts.

Cheesy Scalloped Potatoes

Cooking time: 6 to 8 hours on LOW   3 to 4 hours on HIGH
Attention: Minimal

Potatoes win, hands down, as just about everyone's favorite food. They're easy to cook, nutritious, and, best of all, tasty!

   5 large **potatoes**, peeled and cut into $1/2$-inch (6-mm) slices

   1 large **onion**, cut into $1/2$-inch (13-mm) rings

   Salt and freshly ground black pepper

   Two $10^3/4$-ounce (305-g) cans **condensed cheddar cheese soup**

Spray the inside of the slow cooker with cooking spray.

Place one-third of the potato slices in the slow cooker and spread them out evenly. Top the potato slices with half of the onion rings and sprinkle the onion rings with salt and pepper to taste. Layer on another third of the potato slices and the remainder of the onion rings, and season the mixture with more salt and pepper. Add the rest of the potato slices, then pour the condensed soup over everything. Cover and cook on LOW for 6 to 8 hours or on HIGH for 3 to 4 hours, or until the potato slices are tender.

Before serving, stir the mixture and season it with additional salt and pepper to taste.

YIELD: 6 servings

NUTRITIONAL ANALYSIS: One serving of the basic recipe contains 191 calories; 7 g fat; 6 g protein; 27 g carbohydrate; and 3 g dietary fiber.

IT'S GOOD FOR YOU

Potatoes may be the latest health foods! Scientists recently discovered that chemicals in potatoes called kukoamines lowered blood pressure.

Cheesy Hash Browns

Cooking time: 4 1/2 to 6 1/2 hours
Attention: Add another ingredient during final 30 minutes

Nothing beats a cheesy hash-brown casserole as comfort food. The flavors meld, and the result is nothing short of magic.

One 32-ounce (905-g) bag frozen **hash brown potatoes**, partially thawed

1 teaspoon (6 g) salt

1/2 teaspoon freshly ground black pepper

Two 10 3/4-ounce (305-g) cans **condensed cheddar cheese soup**

1 cup (230 g) **sour cream**

Spray the slow cooker with cooking spray.

Put the partially thawed hash browns in the slow cooker and spread them out evenly. Sprinkle them with the salt and pepper, then top them with the condensed soup. Cover and cook on LOW for 4 to 6 hours, stirring occasionally.

A half hour before the dish is done, add the sour cream and stir to combine. Cook for an additional 30 minutes, or until the mixture is thoroughly heated.

YIELD: 10 servings

ADD IT! For a richer casserole, add 1/2 cup (25 g) sliced scallions and 3 tablespoons (42 g) butter, melted, to the soup. Add 1 cup (130 g) frozen peas to the mixture an hour before serving it, and garnish the finished dish with 1/2 cup (56 g) shredded cheddar cheese.

NUTRITIONAL ANALYSIS: One serving of the basic recipe contains 186 calories; 10 g fat; 5 g protein; 21 g carbohydrate; and 2 g dietary fiber.

TRY THIS

This dish is perfect for a homestyle supper with fried chicken, green beans, and good old-fashioned Jell-O for dessert. Or take it to your next potluck or church supper!

Easy Cheesy Potato Casserole

Cooking time: 6 ½ to 8 ½ hours on LOW   3 ½ to 4 ½ hours on HIGH
Attention: Add more ingredients during final 15 to 30 minutes

Home-style good! The creamy potato flavor and tasty hash browns are enhanced by the melted cheddar.

> One 24-ounce (680-g) bag frozen Southern-style chunky **hash brown potatoes**, partially thawed
>
> One 10¾-ounce (305-g) **can condensed cream of potato soup**
>
> Salt and freshly ground black pepper
>
> 1 cup (113 g) grated **cheddar cheese**

Put the partially thawed hash browns and condensed soup in the slow cooker and stir to combine. Cover and cook on LOW for 6 to 8 hours or on HIGH for 3 to 4 hours.

Stir the mixture, season it with salt and pepper to taste, and sprinkle it with the grated cheese. Cover and cook for another 15 to 30 minutes, or until the cheese has melted.

YIELD: 10 servings

ADD IT! Stir 1 pound (455 g) ham or sausage, chopped, and 1 cup (150 g) frozen peas, thawed, into the hash-brown mixture.

NUTRITIONAL ANALYSIS: One serving of the basic recipe contains 116 calories; 5 g fat; 5 g protein; 15 g carbohydrate; and 1 g dietary fiber.

TRY THIS

Crank up the heat by using grated pepper jack cheese instead of the cheddar, and adding a few drops of hot sauce (red or the milder jalapeno green) to taste.

🏺 Au Gratin Potatoes

Cooking time: 7 to 9 hours on LOW   3 1/2 to 4 1/2 hours on HIGH
Attention: Minimal

Another successful pairing of hash browns and cheesy goodness. Enjoy with breakfast, lunch, or dinner.

Two 10 3/4-ounce (305-g) cans **condensed cheddar cheese soup**

One 13-ounce (390-ml) can **evaporated milk**

One 32-ounce (905-g) bag frozen **hash brown potatoes**, partially thawed

Salt and freshly ground black pepper

Spray the inside of the slow cooker with cooking spray.

Put the condensed soup and evaporated milk in the slow cooker and stir to combine. Add the partially thawed hash browns and stir again. Cover and cook on LOW for 7 to 9 hours or on HIGH for 3 1/2 to 4 1/2 hours.

Before serving, stir the mixture and season it with salt and pepper to taste.

YIELD: 10 servings

ADD IT! Garnish the dish with canned french-fried onion rings just before serving it.

NUTRITIONAL ANALYSIS: One serving of the basic recipe contains 186 calories; 8 g fat; 7 g protein; 24 g carbohydrate; and 2 g dietary fiber.

TRY THIS

You can substitute 10 thinly sliced or cubed baking potatoes for the hash browns in this recipe if you wish.

🏺 Rustic Mashed Potatoes

Cooking time: 6 to 8 hours on LOW   3 to 4 hours on HIGH
Attention: Minimal

An elegant pairing with any entrée. You can't fail to enjoy the rich flavor of slow-cooked, mashed potatoes.

8 baking **potatoes**, cut into 1/2-inch (1.3-cm) cubes

1/4 cup (60 ml) water

2 tablespoons (28 g) **butter**, cut into small pieces

1 1/4 (8 g) teaspoons salt

1/4 teaspoon freshly ground black pepper

3/4 to 1 cup (175 to 235 ml) **milk**

Put the potato cubes, water, butter, salt, and pepper in the slow cooker and mix well. Cover and cook on LOW for 6 to 8 hours or on HIGH for 3 to 4 hours, or until the potatoes are tender.

Add the milk to the slow cooker and mash the potato mixture with a potato masher or electric mixer until it is smooth.

YIELD: 8 servings

ADD IT! Add 2 cloves garlic, minced.

NUTRITIONAL ANALYSIS: One serving of the basic recipe (made with 1 cup milk) contains 190 calories; 4 g fat; 5 g protein; 35 g carbohydrate; and 3 g dietary fiber.

TRY THIS

Use sweet potatoes in place of baking potatoes in this dish for a delicious change of pace. Perfect with ham, roast pork, fried chicken or fish!

🍲 Smashed Garlic Potatoes

Cooking time: 7 to 9 hours on LOW   3 1/2 to 4 1/2 hours on HIGH
Attention: Minimal

Tender, garlicky—delicious! These potatoes make a stylish appearance next to green vegetables and a steak, be it beef or salmon.

 3 pounds (1.4 kg) **white potatoes**, cut into cubes of uniform size

 1/2 cup (120 ml) water

 2 tablespoons plus 1 teaspoon (28 g) minced **garlic in olive oil**, undrained

 1 teaspoon (6 g) salt

 1/4 to 1/2 cup (60 to 120 ml) **milk**

Put the potato cubes, water, garlic with olive oil, and salt in the slow cooker and mix well. Cover and cook on LOW for 7 to 9 hours or on HIGH for 3 1/2 to 4 1/2 hours, or until the potatoes are tender.

Add 1/2 cup of the milk and mash the potatoes coarsely. Continue mashing the potatoes and adding milk until the desired consistency is achieved.

Serve the potatoes immediately or keep them warm in the slow cooker for up to 2 hours.

YIELD: 10 servings

ADD IT! Add 4 ounces (115 g) cream cheese with onion and chives just before adding the milk.

NUTRITIONAL ANALYSIS: One serving of the basic recipe (made with 1/2 cup milk) contains 122 calories; 1 g fat; 3 g protein; 26 g carbohydrate; and 2 g dietary fiber.

⛉ Baked Sweet Potatoes

Cooking time: 4 to 6 hours   **Attention:** Minimal

Sweet potatoes are fabulously nutritious and have no added calories or fats when baked. Enjoy straight from the slow cooker, add a dollop of whipped butter, or slather on the brown sugar and honey.

5 medium **sweet potatoes**, unpeeled, scrubbed well but not dried

Put the damp sweet potatoes in the slow cooker. Cover and cook on LOW for 4 to 6 hours. The baking time will depend on the sizes of the sweet potatoes. Sweet potatoes of uniform size will be done at the same time.

YIELD: 5 servings

NUTRITIONAL ANALYSIS: One serving of the basic recipe contains 137 calories; .4 g fat; 2 g protein; 32 g carbohydrate; and 4 g dietary fiber.

DID YOU KNOW?

Many people call sweet potatoes—especially the orange-fleshed kinds—yams, but a yam is really a tropical root, while a sweet potato is actually an enlarged underground stem called a rhizome. That's why when you put a sweet potato into a glass of water, leaves sprout from the top and roots grow down into the water.

🍲 Maple-Apple Sweet Potatoes

Cooking time: 6 to 8 hours on LOW   3 to 4 hours on HIGH
Attention: Minimal

Tender potatoes drip with the sweetness of a maple-apple glaze. Suitable to sit alongside any main course. Serve with the maple-apple syrup spooned over the potatoes.

> 1/4 cup (81 g) pure **maple syrup**
>
> 1/4 cup (60 ml) **apple juice**
>
> 4 small **sweet potatoes**, peeled and quartered
>
> Salt

Put the maple syrup and apple juice in the slow cooker and mix well. Add the quartered sweet potatoes and stir to coat them. Cover and cook on LOW for 6 to 8 hours or on HIGH for 3 to 4 hours, or until the potatoes are fork-tender.

Before serving, stir the mixture and season it with salt to taste.

YIELD: 4 servings

ADD IT! Stir in 1 tablespoon (14 g) butter just before seasoning the potatoes with the salt.

NUTRITIONAL ANALYSIS: One serving of the basic recipe contains 195 calories; .5 g fat; 2 g protein; 47 g carbohydrate; and 4 g dietary fiber.

IT'S GOOD FOR YOU

Sweet potatoes are excellent sources of vitamin A (as beta-carotene) and are good sources of vitamin C and manganese. They're rich in antioxidants, and have recently been classified as an "antidiabetic" food because they help stabilize blood sugar and lower insulin resistance.

🥣 Candied Sweet Potatoes

Cooking time: 6 to 8 hours on LOW   3 to 4 hours on HIGH
Attention: Minimal

Candied Sweet Potatoes and the slow cooker are a fabulous combination, as you can cook, warm, and serve in the same dish. That's key when trying to manage your holiday kitchen.

> Two 15-ounce (417-g) cans cut **sweet potatoes** in light syrup, undrained
>
> ¼ cup (56 g) **brown sugar**, packed
>
> 4 tablespoons (55 g) **butter**, melted
>
> 1 teaspoon (6 g) salt
>
> ⅛ teaspoon freshly ground black pepper

Put the sweet potatoes in the slow cooker and mash them with a potato masher. Combine the brown sugar, melted butter, salt, and pepper in a small bowl and pour the mixture over the mashed sweet potatoes. Cover and cook on LOW for 6 to 8 hours or on HIGH for 3 to 4 hours.

YIELD: 8 servings

NUTRITIONAL ANALYSIS: One serving of the basic recipe contains 192 calories; 49 g fat; 1 g protein; 34 g carbohydrate; and 3 g dietary fiber.

TRY THIS

Your Candied Sweet Potatoes will pack a holiday punch if you add a splash of brandy or bourbon along with the brown sugar, melted butter, and seasonings. Garnish the dish with chopped nuts or marshmallows.

🍴 Peachy Sweet Potatoes

Cooking time: 5 to 7 hours on LOW   2 1/2 to 3 1/2 hours on HIGH
Attention: Minimal

A refreshing change from brown sugar and butter. Even people who don't particularly care for sweet potatoes love these.

  6 **sweet potatoes**, peeled and cut into 1/2-inch (1.3-cm) chunks

  1 cup (262 g) **peach pie filling**

  1 teaspoon finely minced fresh **ginger**

  1/4 teaspoon salt

  1/4 teaspoon freshly ground black pepper

Spray the inside of the slow cooker with cooking spray.

Put the sweet potato chunks, pie filling, minced ginger, salt, and pepper in the slow cooker and mix well. Cover and cook on LOW for 5 to 7 hours or on HIGH for 2 1/2 to 3 1/2 hours, or until the sweet potatoes are fork-tender.

YIELD: 6 servings

ADD IT! Garnish the dish with 1/2 cup (55 g) chopped pecans or walnuts.

NUTRITIONAL ANALYSIS: One serving of the basic recipe contains 137 calories; .3 g fat; 2 g protein; 32 g carbohydrate; and 4 g dietary fiber.

TRY THIS

Enjoy these with apple pie filling and a teaspoon of ground cinnamon instead of the peach pie filling and grated ginger.

☙ Orange Sweet Potatoes

Cooking time: 6 to 8 hours on LOW   3 to 4 hours on HIGH
Attention: Minimal

Here's another change-of-pace recipe for sweet potatoes. Orange juice makes it zesty.

Two 15-ounce (417-g) cans cut **sweet potatoes** in light syrup, drained

1 cup (284 g) frozen **orange juice concentrate**

3/4 cup (169 g) **brown sugar**, packed

Salt and freshly ground black pepper

Spray the inside of the slow cooker with cooking spray.

Put the drained sweet potato pieces in the slow cooker.

In a large saucepan over medium-low heat, cook the frozen orange juice concentrate and brown sugar until thickened. Pour the sauce over the sweet potatoes. Cover and cook on LOW for 6 to 8 hours or on HIGH for 3 to 4 hours.

Before serving, stir the mixture and season it with salt and pepper to taste.

YIELD: 8 servings

ADD IT! Add 1/2 teaspoon ground nutmeg along with the salt and pepper, and garnish the dish with 1/2 cup (55 g) chopped pecans.

NUTRITIONAL ANALYSIS: One serving of the basic recipe contains 249 calories; .4 g fat; 2 g protein; 61 g carbohydrate; and 4 g dietary fiber.

TRY THIS

For a classic sweet potato casserole, skip the salt and pepper and cover the top of the dish with mini-marshmallows when you're ready to serve it. Serve as soon as the marshmallows melt.

🍶 Simple White Rice

Cooking time: 6 to 8 hours
Attention: Minimal

No peeking allowed! This rice cooks itself to perfection, as long as you don't lift the lid.

2 1/4 cups (529 ml) water

1 cup (185 g) raw **long-grain converted rice**

3 tablespoons (42 g) **margarine**

1/2 to 1 tablespoon (2 to 4 g) dried or minced **fresh parsley**

1 teaspoon salt

Spray the inside of the slow cooker with cooking spray.

Put the water, raw rice, margarine, parsley, and salt in the slow cooker and stir to combine. Cover and cook on LOW for 6 to 8 hours, or just until the rice is tender.

YIELD: 6 servings

ADD IT! Add 1/4 teaspoon freshly ground black pepper.

NUTRITIONAL ANALYSIS: One serving of the basic recipe contains 163 calories; 6 g fat; 2 g protein; 25 g carbohydrate; and .3 g dietary fiber.

TRY THIS

Substitute chopped fresh chives or mint for the parsley for a refreshingly different taste.

 Yellow Rice

You can't beat Yellow Rice with black beans or roast pork. Add fried plantains and café con leche for a virtual trip to Cuba.

2 1/4 cups (529 ml) water

1 cup (185 g) raw **long-grain converted rice**

2 1/2 tablespoons (35 ml) **olive oil**

1/2 teaspoon **saffron threads**

1 teaspoon salt

1/4 teaspoon freshly ground black pepper

Spray the inside of the slow cooker with cooking spray.

Put the water, raw rice, olive oil, saffron threads, salt, and pepper in the slow cooker and stir well. Cover and cook on LOW for 6 to 8 hours, or just until the rice is tender. Resist the urge to lift the lid while the rice is cooking!

YIELD: 6 servings

NUTRITIONAL ANALYSIS: One serving of the basic recipe contains 163 calories; 6 g fat; 2 g protein; 25 g carbohydrate; and .5 g dietary fiber.

TRY THIS

To turn your Cuban Yellow Rice into Indian Golden Rice, use canola oil, ground turmeric, and black mustard seeds instead of the olive oil, saffron, and black pepper. Add a teaspoon of whole cumin or 1/2 teaspoon of ground cumin and 1/2 teaspoon of ground fenugreek with the other spices, and enjoy your trip to the Far Pavilions!

Chapter 15

• •

Desserts

Who doesn't look forward to dessert? It can be the highlight of the meal or a delicious complement to coffee or tea. Although desserts are not traditionally thought of as slow-cooker fare, many lend themselves well to being cooked, and even served, from the slow cooker. Try our Cherry Cobbler (page 231), Chunky Applesauce (page 242), or Golden Fruit Compote (page 243). Super easy and sinfully delicious. Try a new dessert every night!

Vanilla Upside~Down Cake

Oopsie daisy! We got turned upside down—upside down about everything except the yummy quotient of this cake, served with ice cream or a drizzle of chocolate syrup. Check it out!

> 1 cup (120 g) **all-purpose baking mix**
>
> 1 cup (200 g) **Vanilla Sugar** (page 29)
>
> 1/2 cup (120 ml) **milk**
>
> 1 2/3 cups (392 ml) hot water

Spray the inside of the slow cooker with cooking spray.

Put the baking mix, 1/2 cup (100 g) of the Vanilla Sugar, and the milk in a medium-size bowl and mix well. Spoon the batter evenly into the slow cooker. Mix the remaining 1/2 cup (100 g) of the Vanilla Sugar and the hot water in a separate bowl and pour the mixture over the batter in the slow cooker. Cover and cook on HIGH for 2 to 3 hours, or until the center of the cake springs back when pressed.

Scoop the cake out of the slow cooker and serve it with whipped cream, chocolate sauce, or ice cream.

YIELD: 8 servings

NUTRITIONAL ANALYSIS: One serving of the basic recipe contains 166 calories; 3 g fat; 2 g protein; 35 g carbohydrate; and .4 g dietary fiber.

TRY THIS

To make a Chocolate Upside-Down Cake, mix 3 tablespoons (15 g) unsweetened cocoa into the baking mix and 1/3 cup (27 g) cocoa into the Vanilla Sugar-hot water mixture.

🥣 Cherry Cobbler

Cooking time: 3 to 4 hours on LOW   1 1/2 to 2 hours on HIGH
Attention: Minimal

This cobbler is super simple, so you may find yourself preparing it frequently. Or will that be because it's simply delicious?

One 21-ounce (595-g) can **cherry pie filling**

One 18 1/2-ounce (511-g) box **yellow cake mix**

4 tablespoons (55 g) **butter**, melted

Put the pie filling in the slow cooker and spread it out evenly. In a medium-size bowl, stir the cake mix and melted butter until a crumbly mixture forms, then sprinkle the mixture over the pie filling. Cover and cook on LOW for 3 to 4 hours or on HIGH for 1 1/2 to 2 hours.

YIELD: 8 servings

ADD IT! Sprinkle 1/2 cup (55 g) chopped pecans over the crumb mixture before cooking the cake.

NUTRITIONAL ANALYSIS: One serving of the basic recipe contains 416 calories; 13 g fat; 3 g protein; 72 g carbohydrate; and 1 g dietary fiber.

TRY THIS

Substitute blueberry or apple pie filling for the cherry filling to vary the flavor of this fun, easy dessert. Serve all the flavors with vanilla ice cream or whipped cream (or both!).

🥣 Peach Cobbler

Cooking time: 1 1/2 to 2 hours
Attention: Remove cover during final 30 minutes

This is a fabulous way to use up leftover biscuits. It's so yummy, you can serve it warm or cold, with or without ice cream. Any way you please, it's a real crowd-pleaser.

5 **biscuits**, each broken into 4 to 6 pieces

One 21-ounce (595-g) can **peach pie filling**

3/4 cup (63 g) crushed cinnamon **graham crackers**

Spray the inside of the slow cooker with cooking spray.

Place half of the biscuit pieces in the slow cooker and spread them out evenly. Spread half of the pie filling over the biscuits and pour half of the crushed graham crackers over the pie filling. Layer on the remaining biscuit pieces, pie filling, and crushed graham crackers. Cover and cook on HIGH for 1 1/2 to 2 hours.

A half hour before the cobbler is done, remove the lid of the slow cooker. Serve the cobbler warm or cold.

YIELD: 6 servings

NUTRITIONAL ANALYSIS: One serving of the basic recipe contains 204 calories; 7 g fat; 4 g protein; 31 g carbohydrate; and 1 g dietary fiber.

TRY THIS

Substitute cinnamon crumb topping for the crushed cinnamon graham crackers. Make your own crumb topping by combining 1/4 cup (56 g) brown sugar, packed; 1/2 teaspoon apple pie spice; and 8 tablespoons (1 stick, or 112 g) butter, softened.

Cinnamon Swirl~Cherry Delight

Cherry and cinnamon are delightful together. A wonderful change-of-pace dessert that's served best in a bowl, with vanilla ice cream.

> One 21-ounce (595-g) can **cherry pie filling**
>
> Half of a 21-ounce (595-g) box **cinnamon swirl cake mix**
>
> 4 tablespoons (55 g) **butter**, melted

Spray the inside of the slow cooker with cooking spray.

Put the pie filling in the slow cooker and spread it out evenly. In a medium-size bowl, stir the cake mix and melted butter until a crumbly mixture forms, then sprinkle the mixture over the pie filling. Cover and cook on LOW for 2 to 3 hours.

Serve the cake at room temperature.

YIELD: 5 servings

ADD IT! Sprinkle 1/4 cup (31 g) slivered almonds over the crumb mixture before cooking the cake.

NUTRITIONAL ANALYSIS: One serving of the basic recipe contains 371 calories; 13 g fat; 2 g protein; 63 g carbohydrate; and 1 g dietary fiber.

TRY THIS

This one's yummy with peach pie filling, too.

Strawberry-Chocolate Crumble

Cooking time: 3 to 4 hours on LOW   1 1/2 to 2 hours on HIGH
Attention: Minimal

Who doesn't go straight for the strawberry and chocolate on the dessert tray? This scrumptious dessert satisfies both cravings, particularly when served with Neapolitan ice cream.

    One 18-ounce (510-g) can **strawberry pie filling**

    One 21-ounce (595-g) box **chocolate cake mix**

    8 tablespoons (1 stick, or 112 g) **butter**, melted

Spray the inside of the slow cooker with cooking spray.

Put the pie filling in the slow cooker and spread it out evenly. In a medium-size bowl, stir the cake mix and melted butter until a crumbly mixture forms, then sprinkle the mixture over the pie filling. Cover and cook on LOW for 3 to 4 hours or on HIGH for 1 1/2 to 2 hours.

Serve the cake at room temperature.

YIELD: 8 servings

ADD IT! Garnish the cake with chocolate curls.

NUTRITIONAL ANALYSIS: One serving of the basic recipe contains 293 calories; 19 g fat; 3 g protein; 33 g carbohydrate; and 1 g dietary fiber.

TRY THIS

Use cherry pie filling instead of strawberry for a rich, luscious flavor. Serve with vanilla or black cherry ice cream.

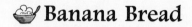Banana Bread

Cooking time: 4 to 6 hours   **Attention:** Minimal

Banana Bread is a delicious side for breakfast, lunch, or dinner. A toasted slice of Banana Bread with butter is fabulous.

> One 8-ounce (225-g) box **banana bread mix**
>
> 1/2 cup (55 g) coarsely **chopped pecans**

Coat the interior of the slow cooker's baking unit with cooking spray, and position the slow cooker's rack on the floor of the machine. If your slow cooker did not come with this equipment, use any baking pan and rack that fit inside the machine.

Prepare the banana bread according to the package directions, stir in pecans, and pour the batter into the pan. Cover the pan and place it on the rack in the slow cooker. Partially cover the slow cooker, propping the lid open with a twist of foil or a wooden skewer to allow the steam to escape, and cook on HIGH for 4 to 6 hours.

Turn the heat OFF and allow the slow cooker to cool for 20 minutes, or until you can remove the pan without burning yourself. Serve the bread warm or at room temperature.

YIELD: 5 servings

NUTRITIONAL ANALYSIS: One serving of the basic recipe contains 251 calories; 12 g fat; 3 g protein; 35 g carbohydrate; and 1 g dietary fiber.

TRY THIS

Turn your banana bread into delicious cake with a cream cheese frosting. To make it, beat a softened (8 oz., 115g) package of cream cheese with 4 tablespoons (55 g) of softened butter and a teaspoon of vanilla with an electric mixer until well blended. Gradually add a box (16 oz., 455 g) of powdered sugar. This recipe makes enough to top two loaves, but you can refrigerate half for a week. Spread the frosting over the cooled loaf or loaves before slicing.

 Crust-Free Cheesecake

Cooking time: 3 to 5 hours   **Attention:** Minimal

This cheesecake has no crust to compete with its delicious flavor. Whether you introduce whipped cream or fruit glaze to the debate is up to you.

12 ounces (340 g) **cream cheese**, softened

½ cup (50 g) **Vanilla Sugar** (page 29)

1 whole **egg** plus 1 egg white

Coat the interior of the slow cooker's baking unit with cooking spray, and position the slow cooker's rack on the floor of the machine. If your slow cooker did not come with this equipment, use any baking pan and rack that fit inside the machine.

Put the softened cream cheese, Vanilla Sugar, whole egg, and egg white in a large bowl and beat with a mixer until well blended; do not overbeat the batter. Pour the batter into the pan and place the pan on the rack in the slow cooker. Cover and cook on HIGH for 3 to 5 hours, or until the sides of the cheesecake look dry and just a little cracked, and its center is firm but still jiggles a bit when shaken.

Turn the heat OFF and allow the slow cooker to cool for 20 minutes, or until you can remove the pan without burning yourself. Run a knife around the edges of the pan to release the cake and to prevent cracks from forming. Allow it to cool completely, then cover it and place it in the refrigerator for at least 3 hours.

To serve the cheesecake, cover the pan with a plate, then carefully invert the pan and let the cheesecake release onto the plate. Place another plate over the cheesecake and invert the cake again, so that the cheesecake is right side up. Garnish the cake with fruit, glaze, or whipped topping, or just slice, serve, and enjoy it.

YIELD: 10 servings

NUTRITIONAL ANALYSIS: One serving of the basic recipe contains 167 calories; 12 g fat; 4 g protein; 11 g carbohydrate; and 0 g dietary fiber.

> **TRY THIS**
> Pour the batter into a graham cracker pie shell in a pie pan, and bake it as directed above.

Rice Pudding

Making Rice Pudding doesn't have to be a production. With three ingredients commonly found in the kitchen, you can have a warm and comforting dessert.

2 1/2 cups (413 g) cooked **rice**

One 14-ounce (398-g) can **sweetened condensed milk**

3 **eggs**, well beaten

Spray the inside of the slow cooker with cooking spray.

Put the cooked rice, condensed milk, and beaten eggs in the slow cooker and stir well. Cover and cook on LOW for 4 to 6 hours, stirring only once, after 1 hour.

Serve the pudding warm or cold.

YIELD: 6 servings

NUTRITIONAL ANALYSIS: One serving of the basic recipe contains 349 calories; 9 g fat; 11 g protein; 58 g carbohydrate; and .3 g dietary fiber.

TRY THIS

For a richer, more traditional pudding, add 3/4 cup (109 g) raisins; 2 tablespoons (28 g) butter, melted; 1 teaspoon vanilla extract (5 ml); and 1/8 teaspoon ground nutmeg.

Baked Apples with Raisins

Serve these apples warm or chilled, along with a selection of cheeses.

 6 baking **apples**, cored

 ¹/2 cup (73 g) **raisins**

 1 cup (189 g) **Cinnamon Sugar** (page 29)

 1 cup (235 ml) hot water

Place the cored apples upright in the slow cooker. Fill the center of each apple with one-sixth of the raisins. In a small bowl, combine the water and Cinnamon Sugar, then pour the mixture over the apples. Cover and cook on LOW for 3 to 5 hours.

YIELD: 6 servings

ADD IT! Add 2 tablespoons (28 g) butter, melted, and ¹/2 teaspoon apple pie spice to the Cinnamon Sugar-hot water mixture.

NUTRITIONAL ANALYSIS: One serving of the basic recipe contains 237 calories; .7 g fat; .7 g protein; 62 g carbohydrate; and 6 g dietary fiber.

TRY THIS

Use apple cider instead of water for a richer flavor. Serve hot with vanilla ice cream.

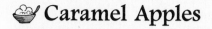 Caramel Apples

Cooking time: 1 to 1 1/2 hours   **Attention:** Stir frequently

An eternal favorite that evokes memories of fall carnivals and fairs. You can easily halve this recipe, but you'd end up with just half the fun.

- 8 **wooden sticks**
- 8 **medium apples**, washed and dried
- 2 pounds (910 g) **caramel candies**
- 1/4 cup (60 ml) water

Insert a stick into the stem end of each apple. Line the counter with enough waxed paper to hold all the apples.

Combine the caramels and water in the slow cooker. Cover and cook on HIGH for 1 to 1 1/2 hours, stirring frequently.

Turn the heat to LOW. When the slow cooker has cooled enough to allow you to work without burning yourself, dip an apple into the hot caramel, turning the apple to coat it all the way around. Try to dip the apple up to the stick, but be careful not to burn yourself on the edge of the slow cooker. Let the excess caramel drip back into the slow cooker, then set the apple down to cool on the waxed paper. Repeat with the remaining apples.

YIELD: 8 servings

NUTRITIONAL ANALYSIS: One serving of the basic recipe contains 562 calories; 13 g fat; 5 g protein; 118 g carbohydrate; and 5 g dietary fiber.

TRY THIS

Make your own caramel-apple dip by putting the caramel candies and water into the slow cooker with 2 tablespoons (28 g) of melted butter. Stir to mix when the caramels have melted. When the slow cooker has cooled but the mixture is still melted, dip apple slices into the caramel and enjoy. Crisp apples like Granny Smith taste best.

Hot Spiced Pears

For centuries, people have enjoyed the spicy goodness of baked pears. This luscious dessert is flavorful enough to stand alone, but it's also fabulous served over waffles, pancakes, pound cake, or ice cream.

> 8 **pears**, peeled, cored, and sliced
>
> One 8-ounce (225-g) can **pineapple chunks**, undrained
>
> 1 tablespoon (7 g) **apple pie spice**

Put the pear slices, pineapple chunks, pineapple juice, and apple pie spice in the slow cooker and stir to combine. Cover and cook on LOW for 8 to 10 hours.

Stir the mixture again and serve it warm or cold.

YIELD: 8 servings

NUTRITIONAL ANALYSIS: One serving of the basic recipe contains 117 calories; .8 g fat; .8 g protein; 30 g carbohydrate; and 5 g dietary fiber.

TRY THIS

Add ¼ cup (36 g) raisins, and substitute apples or peaches for half of the pears. Top with whipped cream or ice cream.

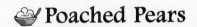 Poached Pears

Cooking time: 3 1/2 to 4 hours | **Attention:** Minimal

These raspberry-and-cinnamon-infused pears taste as good as they look. Enjoy them chilled, with gingerbread and whipped cream.

- 1 1/2 quarts (1.4 ml) **cranberry-raspberry juice**
- 1/4 cup (47 g) **Cinnamon Sugar** (page 29)
- 5 firm **pears**, peeled and cored but with the stem intact

Put the cranberry-raspberry juice and Cinnamon Sugar in the slow cooker and stir until the sugar has dissolved. Add the pears, submerging them in the juice mixture. Cover and cook on LOW for 3 1/2 to 4 hours, or until the pears are tender.

Turn the heat OFF and allow the slow cooker to cool for 20 minutes, or until the pears are safe enough to handle. Remove the pears and syrup from the slow cooker and refrigerate them until they're very cold.

Serve the pears chilled, in shallow bowls, drizzled with the syrup.

YIELD: 5 servings

NUTRITIONAL ANALYSIS: One serving of the basic recipe contains 326 calories; .6 g fat; .6 g protein; 82 g carbohydrate; and 4 g dietary fiber.

TRY THIS

Substitute your favorite white, blush, or red wine for up to 2 cups (470 ml) of the juice. Garnish the dish with fresh raspberries.

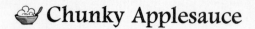 Chunky Applesauce

Cooking time: 4 to 6 hours   **Attention:** Minimal

It's fun and easy to make your own mouth-watering applesauce. Serve it warm, or chill it first.

    6 large cooking **apples**, peeled, cored, and cut into chunks of uniform size

    1/2 to 3/4 cup (95 to 142 g) **Cinnamon Sugar** (page 29)

    1/2 teaspoon ground **nutmeg**

    1/4 cup (60 ml) water

Put the apple chunks, Cinnamon Sugar, ground nutmeg, and water in the slow cooker and stir to combine. Cover and cook on LOW for 4 to 6 hours.

Before serving, stir the applesauce and add more Cinnamon Sugar to taste.

YIELD: 6 servings

NUTRITIONAL ANALYSIS: One serving of the basic recipe (made with 1/2 cup Cinnamon Sugar) contains 142 calories; .7 g fat; .3 g protein; 37 g carbohydrate; and 4 g dietary fiber.

TRY THIS

Substitute apple cider for the water for a richer taste. You'll also get a richer flavor if you use a mix of apple varieties instead of just one type.

Golden Fruit Compote

Cooking time: 8 to 10 hours

Attention: Stir every 2 hours; add water as necessary

This compote is as delightfully fruity as it's pretty when served cold with white cake, pound cake, or vanilla ice cream. It's also wonderful served warm as an alternative to cranberry sauce.

Two 20-ounce (570-g) cans **pineapple chunks**, undrained

One 15-ounce (417-g) package **golden raisins** or **dried mixed apples, peaches, and apricots**

1 cup (120 ml) water

½ teaspoon **apple pie spice**

Put the pineapple chunks, raisins, water, and apple pie spice in the slow cooker and stir to combine. Cover and cook on LOW for 8 to 10 hours, or until the flavors have melded and the mixture has become very thick, stirring every 2 hours and adding water as needed.

YIELD: 10 servings

ADD IT! Substitute apple juice for the water.

NUTRITIONAL ANALYSIS: One serving of the basic recipe (made with golden raisins) contains 197 calories; .3 g fat; 2 g protein; 52 g carbohydrate; and 3 g dietary fiber.

DID YOU KNOW?

"Compote," which we know as a thick fruit stew, is derived from the Old French composte, from Latin compostus, which, as you might guess, is also the basis of our word "compost." What do they have in common? They're both mixtures, the meaning of the original Latin word.

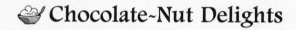 Chocolate-Nut Delights

Cooking time: 45 to 75 minutes   **Attention:** Stir every 15 minutes

Indulge your love affair with chocolate—create decadent delights using chocolate and your favorite nuts. Set the mood by serving them in petite, lacy baking cups on an embellished silver tray.

> 1 ½ pounds (683 g) semisweet **baking chocolate**, coarsely chopped
>
> 1 pound (455 g) **white chocolate squares**, coarsely chopped
>
> Two 10-ounce (280-g) cans deluxe **mixed nuts** or your favorite nuts

Spray the inside of the slow cooker with cooking spray. Line the counter with enough waxed paper to hold all the nut clusters while they harden.

Put the semisweet baking chocolate and white chocolate in the slow cooker. Cover and cook on LOW for 45 to 75 minutes, or until the chocolate melts, stirring every 15 minutes.

Add the nuts and mix well. Turn the heat OFF and allow the mixture to cool slightly, then use a tablespoon to drop it in 1 ½-inch (3.8-cm) mounds onto the waxed paper. Allow the nut clusters to cool and harden.

Store the nut clusters at room temperature in an airtight container.

YIELD: 36 nut clusters

TIP: Make sure not to overheat the chocolate, which melts better and faster at lower temperatures. Be extremely careful not to allow even a drop of water into the slow cooker or the chocolate will seize and become grainy. A little vegetable oil will restore the chocolate, but it will also affect the flavor.

NUTRITIONAL ANALYSIS: One serving of the basic recipe (made with mixed nuts) contains 251 calories; 19 g fat; 4 g protein; 23 g carbohydrate; and 2 g dietary fiber.

DID YOU KNOW?

Chocolate is a multibillion-dollar industry in the United States, but it wasn't always that way. Chocolate started out as a beverage used by the indigenous peoples of South America, evolved into a fashionable drink favored by the elite of Europe, and was finally used, in the mid-1800s, to make the superbly edible confections enjoyed today.

White Chocolate~Macadamia Nut Clusters

Pure decadence—macadamia nuts and white chocolate in a mantle of semi-sweet chocolate. Enjoy alone or with a splash of gourmet Hawaiian coffee.

1 1/2 pounds (683 g) semisweet **chocolate candy melts**

Two 6-ounce (168-g) cans whole **macadamia nuts**

1/4 cup (43 g) **white chocolate chips**

Spray the inside of the slow cooker with cooking spray. Line the counter with enough waxed paper to hold all the nut clusters while they harden.

Put the candy melts in the slow cooker. Cover and cook on LOW for 45 to 75 minutes, or until the chocolate melts, stirring every 15 minutes.

Turn the heat OFF, add the macadamia nuts and white chocolate chips, and mix well. (The white chocolate chips should not melt.) Allow the mixture to cool slightly, then use a tablespoon to drop it in 1 1/2-inch (3.8-cm) mounds onto the waxed paper. Allow it to cool completely and set.

Store the nut clusters at room temperature in an airtight container.

YIELD: 36 nut clusters

NUTRITIONAL ANALYSIS: One serving of the basic recipe contains 251 calories; 19 g fat; 4 g protein; 23 g carbohydrate; and 2 g dietary fiber.

DID YOU KNOW?

Candy melts are easier to melt than baking chocolate because they're made using a special manufacturing process. They're a combination of cocoa, sugar, milk solids, vegetable oil, flavorings, and color.

Resources for Slow Cooking

The resurgence in slow cooking leaves us with a plethora of resources on the Internet.

Food Safety

Knowledge of how to properly handle, prepare, cook, and store food is a must for all who eat.

Eat Well, Eat Safe
www.eatwelleatsafe.ca/newindex2.htm
Information on eating well and eating safely from the Food Safety Network.

"Focus On: Slow Cooker Safety"
www.fsis.usda.gov/Fact_Sheets/Focus_On_Slow_Cooker_
    Safety/index.asp
The slow-cooker safety webpage of the USDA Food Safety and Inspection Service.

Foodlink
www.foodlink.org.uk
A complete guide to food safety, United Kingdom style.

Gateway to Government Food Safety Information
www.foodsafety.gov
Food-safety guidelines and information from the U.S. government.

Partnership for Food Safety Education
www.fightbac.org/main.cfm
The Partnership for Food Safety's site providing information for educators, the media, and consumers.

"Slow Cooker Food Safety"
http://cufan.clemson.edu/hgic/factsheets/hgic3585.htm
Slow-cooker food-safety webpage of the Home and Garden Information Center, Extension Service, Clemson University.

Slow~Cooker Recipe Sites

Some very informative sites where the overwhelming number of recipes have more than three ingredients.

Chef Mom
http://chefmom.myria.com/recipebox/Specialties/
    Slow_Cooker
Recipes from a mother's point of view.

Crockpot Kitchen
www.crockpot.cdkitchen.com
A huge site with recipes, tips, games, a glossary, and more.

"Slow Cooker: One Pot and Walk Away"
www.mccormick.com/content.cfm?ID=10100
McCormick's recipes for slow cookers.

"Southern U.S. Cuisine: Crockpot and Slow Cooker Recipes Index"
http://southernfood.about.com/library/crock/blcpidx.htm
A huge index of slow-cooker recipes and resources offered by About.com.

Slow~Cooker Products and Reviews

For when you're in the market for a new slow cooker or just want to check out what the experts have to say about your present model.

ConsumerSearch
www.consumersearch.com/www/kitchen/slow_cookers/
A comprehensive review of the slow cookers currently on the market. It also reviews the reviewers and lists slow-cooker recalls.

"Crock Pot"
www.crockpot.com
The Rival slow-cooker product page. You can purchase accessories from this site.

"In the Kitchen: Slow-Cooker Supremes"
http://magazines.ivillage.com/goodhousekeeping/
    consumer/kitchen/articles/0,,284514_664621,00.html
Good Housekeeping's 2005 slow-cooker product reviews on iVillage.

"Slow Cookers"
http://hamiltonbeach.com/products/slowcookers/
    main.html
The Hamilton Beach slow-cooker product page.

U.S. Consumer Product Safety Commission
www.cpsc.gov
Slow-cooker recalls, product safety news, and reports of unsafe products.

"West Bend Slow Cookers"
www.westbend.com/slow-cookers.htm
West Bend's slow-cooker product page, which contains links to lots of slow-cooker and other small-appliance information.

Mail~Order and Internet Purchasing

Mail-order and online resources for purchasing special ingredients.

Albertsons Web Site
www.albertsons.com/delivery.asp
For online shopping from Albertsons supermarket chain, with delivery service available in 14 large U.S. cities and metropolitan areas.

Campbell's Web Site
www.campbellsoup.com
For soups, pasta sauces, juices, salsa, and broth.

Del Monte Web Site
www.delmonte.com/Home.asp
For specialty canned vegetable blends.

Emeril's Web Site
www.emerilstore.com
For spices, rubs, pasta sauces, salsa, and more from Chef Emeril Lagasse.

Fantastic Foods Web Site
www.fantasticfoods.com
For delicious and innovative vegetarian food choices.

Green Giant Web Site
www.greengiant.com
For frozen vegetable blends and specialty canned vegetables.

Heinz Web Site

www.heinz.com

For the many multi-ingredient brands of Heinz, including pasta sauces, steak sauces, and hash brown potatoes, to name a few.

IronQ Web Site

ironq.com

For cooking sauces and more, including Iron Chef-brand products.

Lawry's Web Site

www.lawrys.com

For spice blends, seasoning mixes, sauces, and marinades.

Made in California

www.madeincalifornia.net

For gourmet foods, including Bella Sun Luci Sun Dried Tomatoes in 100% olive oil and herbs.

McCormick Web Site

www.mccormick.com

For gravies, sauces, seasonings, seasoning blends, and gourmet items from McCormick.

Netgrocer

www.netgrocer.com

For multi-ingredient products delivered to your door.

Newman's Own Web Site

www.newmansown.com

For spaghetti sauces, dressings, salsa, and more.

PictSweet Web Site

www.pictsweet.com

For premium frozen vegetables and blends.

Ragú Web Site

www.eat.com/products/products.asp

For links to all the Ragú brands. Check out all the flavors!

"Secrets to Cooking Tex-Mex Food Items"

www.texmex.net/products/foods.htm

For Ro-Tel products, to add zest to any dish calling for tomatoes.

Smucker's Web Site

www.smuckers.com

For Smuckers' yummy flavorings.

Wyler's Web Site

www.wylers.com

For bouillon and soup mixes.

Index

Acknowledgments

A big thank-you to my family and all my friends. Writing a cookbook and meeting a deadline didn't leave me much time for socializing or recreation. I am forever thankful to Christina, Clarissa, and Jim, for their love, patience, and encouragement, and (especially to Jim) for the extra responsibility they assumed so that I would be free to write. Thank-you also to Bonnie, April, Carol, and Marcia, who listened tirelessly, and to my supportive friends at my "day job," who provided encouragement, insight, and recipe suggestions, plus didn't mind too much when I had to work through lunch. Thank-you to Anthony, for his encouragement, advice, time, and proofreading skills. Thanks also to Ellen Phillips and Elaine Will Sparber, for their editorial assistance and for guiding this project with good humor, diligence, and sensitivity. When time was short, their tempers weren't.

I am so very grateful and blessed to have every one of you in my life.

About the Author

Suzanne Bonet is a technical writer and a mother of two residing in the Gulf Coast region of Florida, in scenic Tampa Bay. Food and technical writing have long been entwined in her life. She learned the importance of well-crafted instructions to successful outcomes as a child who baked mounds of cookies, cakes, and pies. As an adult whose day job is writing instructions for using computer applications, her fondness for healthy home cooking and stress-free family dinners led her to depend heavily on her slow cooker—long before its return to "hot" appliance status. Empty nest syndrome inspired her to contemplate writing a slow-cooker cookbook for her girls to take with them to college. From those maternal stirrings evolved the three-ingredient slow-cooker recipe book you hold in your hands today.